GHOST PETS
& SPIRIT
ANIMALS

GHOST PETS & SPIRIT ANIMALS

JILL ARMITAGE

TEMPUS

Dedicated to Jacqui, for your friendship through trying times. Without your help, this book would never have been written. To Sarah, who sorted out all the technical stuff, and to all those wonderful pet owners who opened their hearts and family albums for this book.

First published 2006

Tempus Publishing Limited
The Mill, Brimscombe Port,
Stroud, Gloucestershire, GL5 2QG
www.tempus-publishing.com

British Library Cataloguing in Publication Data.
A catalogue record for this book is available from the British Library.

ISBN 0 7524 3997 9

Typesetting and origination by Tempus Publishing Limited.
Printed in Great Britain.

CONTENTS

Look out for signs that your pet isn't being traumatised by his spirit predecessor.

INTRODUCTION

Jessica was four when Tweet, her budgie died, and arrangements were made to bury him in the garden with all the ceremony befitting a much loved family pet. A suitable-sized shoebox was found, a hole dug in the herbaceous border and the ceremony began. Then Jessica, who had been watching in awed silence, suddenly cried, 'No, don't cover his head or how will he breathe?'

We can smirk at the poignant sentiment of a four-year-old's simple logic, yet as adults don't we also want our beloved pets to live on after death? Some owners believe they actually do because they have experienced seeing or sensing their animals in spirit form. Surprisingly, this is not just a case of wishful thinking on behalf of grieving owners, as cynics would have us believe – this is a fact confirmed by the huge amount of stories that testify to it. What is equally convincing is that all the owners I spoke to had one thing in common: their initial disbelief and the exasperating lack of explanation for what had happened. The main difference seems to be that the ghosts of some animals come back almost immediately to say goodbye, while others still haunt their old homes many years later.

Countless pet owners were eager to share other paranormal experiences that involved their pets, particularly those that defied any conventional explanation. All these stories were given added credibility by their similarity and number and it soon became apparent to me that not only do animals return in spirit form, but that our pets are also very adept at sensing spirits, both animal and human.

Time after time I was told amazing stories of animals that were able to see or sense ghosts, and if it wasn't a ghost what was it? Why would a dog suddenly stand rigid, staring at nothing, its hairs bristling? What would turn a normally placid, playful cat into a spitting, fighting machine that would claw and scratch its owner in its frantic attempt to escape? But escape from what?

Why would a pony avoid a shady area of his field, or horses in a stable make a huge rumpus at exactly the same time that a paranormal investigation being carried out nearby registered a sudden plunge in temperature?

Many of these stories relate to family pets, yet people who have no connection with animals have heard phantom whining, scratching or even snoring. Some individuals have been protected by a guardian angel in canine form, others have met 'The Shuck', a spectral black dog that terrorises country districts, or the hounds from hell that forecast doom and death.

Horses have always been very involved with man, as working animals, transport and pets, so we had to include a selection of stories of people being carried around on ghostly horses, and phantom coaches pulled by headless horses.

Many of these tales have left their mark and found a place in our paranormal folklore. With the current interest in the supernatural, these stories will intrigue and fascinate every animal lover.

Could a cat sense a child's imaginary friend?

I
CAN YOUR PET SEE GHOSTS?

Animals are extremely good as sensing ghosts or spirit presences. They are much more likely to detect a ghost than humans are, but unfortunately we can't interview them to see what they actually see, feel or sense. Luckily, many of us have such an affinity with our pets that we can read their body language, which gives us a pretty good idea when something unusual is taking place.

Can You See What I Can See?

One evening, Jacqui Cooke was alone in the sitting room of her Sheffield home when the door began to slowly open. Thinking it was one of her three dogs, she waited for it to bound in, but when nothing appeared and there was no sound, she went to investigate. She peered into the hall just as a ghostly white shape like a puff of smoke floated along the hall and up the stairs. Rooted to the spot in terror, Jacqui realised that her three dogs, Sheba, Helga and Tarquin, all stood transfixed, silent and alert in the doorway of the kitchen. They too had been watching the apparition and as soon as it disappeared, they all charged into the sitting room.

The Dog who can Sense Spirits

Brenma Howells of Mid-Glamorgan is clairsentient (able to sense spirits) and so too is her German shepherd dog, Remus. When Brenma senses a presence in the house, Remus's ears go up and he sits stock-still.

Remus was still quite young when he began to show signs that as well as being clairsentient, he was also clairvoyant (able to see spirits). According to Brenma, he is never scared and she isn't sure whether he understands the difference between the physical and the spiritual.

...and the Budgie can too

Dogs are not the only animals who can see and sense ghosts. I visited a local psychic in her home a while ago and she took me into her sitting room where a budgie sat in its cage in the corner. It eyed me with interest, but was utterly silent until about five minutes after the psychic had started to talk. Then it started to whistle and chirp. We ignored it, but gradually it got more vocal; its whistles became squawks and squeals and I could stand it no longer. The bird seemed to be in agony.

'Oh he's alright,' said my hostess, seeing my distressed look. 'He always does that when the spirits are present.'

Scared? Me? Do I look scared?

Obedient Judy

Terry Chan began to suspect she had an uninvited spirit visitor in her home because of her Scottie dog Judy. The little dog would stand staring at a particular spot then suddenly sit or beg. Watching her, Terry said Judy behaved as if some invisible person was giving her commands that she was obeying.

The Ghost's Favourite Chair

After the death of his mother, Malcolm Snowdon had the task of disposing of her furniture, but her favourite armchair had special significance and he took it to his home and placed it in the sitting room. Shortly afterwards, he noticed his cat Tabitha behaving strangely and circling the chair in a very odd manner. He picked Tabitha up and sat down on the chair to nurse her, but the cat went crazy. In her attempts to escape, she clawed him as she jumped down and ran out of the room.

From that day on, Tabitha refused to go into the room and every time Malcolm carried her in and placed her anywhere near the chair she always shot out of the door again. Did Tabitha sense the astral presence of Mrs Snowdon in what had been her favourite chair? Most ghosts are known to frequent places, and some do attach themselves to furniture, so it is highly possible.

The Cat that Avoided the Chair

I was told a similar story about a chair that had belonged to the father of a lady who lived in Hathersage. She had acquired her father's chair, and her cat gave it a very wide berth. One day, her cleaning lady was dusting the room and looked up to see a man sitting in the chair. She was so freaked that she ran out of the room and refused to return. Later, when she described the

Above left: The Scottie who obeyed a ghost.

Above right: This photograph was taken in 1891 by Sybell Corbet. The faint figure of a man, particularly the right side of his face and his right hand resting on the chair arm, can be seen sitting in the chair on the left. It is believed to be the ghost of Lord Combermere, a British cavalry commander in the early 1800s. He died in 1891 after being struck by a horse-drawn carriage.

man, the lady of the house showed her a photograph of her late father and she confirmed that it was he who she had seen. It would appear that the family's cat had also seen or sensed the man sitting in the chair which was why he avoided it.

The Cat that Said Goodbye

Whenever Mrs Whiteman visited her son Tom's home, she always made a big fuss of the family cat who reciprocated by brushing round her legs and purring contentedly. The cat would then accompany her to the fireside chair and lie across her feet like a foot warmer. On the day that Mrs Whiteman died, Tom noticed the cat walking round purring contentedly and nodding his head as if rubbing against some invisible object. After a short while, the cat walked over to the fireside chair, paddled around for a few seconds then settled down to lie across the area where he always lay on Mrs Whiteman's feet. It only happened on that one occasion and Tom feels that his mother returned in spirit to say goodbye to her family and her little feline friend.

The Imaginary Friend

Cats and dogs can apparently see or sense ghosts, but this story is rather different because the pet cat obviously shared this ability with the family's three-year-old son. This little boy had an imaginary friend. There's nothing very strange about that, many children do, but this imaginary friend was a lady he called Aunt Anne. There was no Aunt Anne in the family, but this didn't unduly bother the parents until they started to realise that every time their son said that Aunt Anne was there, the family cat started acting very strangely and wanted to be let out of the house. Was the child's imaginary friend an actual ghost that both he and the cat could see?

Does your home house a spirit? Many properties do and animals can sense them.

Was the House Haunted?

Kath and Dennis Dell had just moved into an old house which they were intending to re-vamp. Initially they had been full of enthusiasm but soon Kath was having second thoughts. She sensed a strange atmosphere in the house and although she had never seen anything, she suspected the place was haunted. Then one weekend they had friends to stay and they brought with them their pet dog, Randal. After giving Randal a run round the garden, he was taken into the house where he rushed round sniffing excitedly until he reached the stairs. There he stopped in his tracks, staring up the stairs, his tail between his legs; he let out a deep growl, turned and ran into the kitchen. After that he refused to go any further.

Kath had heard that dogs and cats can sense ghosts, so she decided to experiment and asked another friend if she would bring her cat round. The cat was allowed to roam freely and he meandered round the house quite happily. He even bounded up the stairs, with his mistress and Kath following, but as soon as he entered the main bedroom, he stopped. His back arched, his fur fluffed up and he hissed at something unseen in the corner of the room.

This completely unnerved Kath. She was now sure that her earlier instinct was correct and both animals had seen or sensed something paranormal, but Dennis was unconvinced that the animals' behaviour meant anything of the sort.

Dennis did however agree to ask the neighbours if they could borrow their dog and he told them why. The neighbours listened with interest then told them that an old man had died in the house some time ago and other people living there had also felt his presence. Once Kath had had her gut-feeling confirmed, she arranged for an exorcism, they got on with the re-vamp and lived there for many happy years.

Will our Cat Settle?

A similar story concerned a couple who suspected their house was haunted and didn't like the idea one little bit. After moving in, they had been told that an old man had died there and could not move on until the 'right' people were living in his former home. Obviously they didn't think they were 'the right people', so they put the house on the market, but, having discovered the story, the lady of the house felt duty-bound to inform any prospective buyers of this.

Understandably this made it more difficult to sell. Then one day an elderly couple viewed the property and they liked what they saw. Even the story of the ghost didn't seem to worry them, but they said it might unsettle their pet cat, could they bring it to check?

The cat was small and timid, but he went curiously from room to room and as everyone watched and waited he finally sauntered into the bedroom, then jumped deftly onto the bed. Five minutes later, he was fast asleep in the middle of the duvet and his owners made an offer on the property.

If you are in the process of buying a house, it might be a good idea to introduce your pet to the new home before making the final decision. If he refuses to enter or is wary of any rooms, make a few more enquiries. It may just be stagnant energy but if it is negative think twice.

The Dogs that could Detect a Spirit in the House

A lady who wishes to remain anonymous bought an old house in Brixham that was in such a dreadful state that it took months to get habitable. Then, just when she thought she had got it organised, odd things started to happen.

Sometimes her two dogs would be snoozing or sitting watching television when both their heads would simultaneously turn and stare intently at one place in the room, then both would turn away again at the same time. The lady never saw anything but, observing the peculiar behaviour of her dogs, she had a definite feeling that the house held a spirit presence.

The Frightened Dog

There was one bedroom in her Hertfordshire home where, for many years, Mrs Walker heard strange, inexplicable noises. They were always at around 10.30 p.m. and although Mrs Walker said it sounded like ghostly footsteps, her son tried to persuaded her that it was just old beams creaking.

Is it safe to come out yet?

However she soon noticed that Bruce, her English Springer Spaniel, always avoided this particular bedroom, which was very strange because Bruce bounded about the rest of the house quite freely. It could be her imagination, she thought, but she had to check, so one day as she was about to enter the room, she grabbed hold of Bruce's collar and started to pull him in. The dog instantly pulled back. He struggled and growled until he managed to wriggle out of his collar and, once he had broken free, raced down the stairs and into the garden panic-stricken.

The Fight for Supremacy

Doris Kelley moved house taking her cat Mollie with her. As she stood in the kitchen surveying the scene on her first evening there, she felt something furry rub against her legs. Thinking it was Mollie, she bent down to stroke her, but there was nothing to be seen or felt. Just then Mollie walked into the kitchen and immediately her tail fluffed up and her fur stood on end. She walked round and round some object invisible to Doris in the way she would if inspecting another strange cat. Finally Mollie spat, clawed at something and rushed out of the room. Immediately Doris heard a contented purr and felt the furry object rubbing her legs again.

Next day Mollie disappeared and the only explanation Doris could find was that the phantom cat had proved to be so dominant and determined to remain the solo, resident cat, that Mollie had been forced to leave.

Plato Fights his Spirit Predecessor

Richard Low was returning to his bungalow home one day when, as he entered the front door, he saw the back end of a German shepherd dog disappearing down the hall and into the spare bedroom. That door was normally kept closed, particularly at the moment because they had a young German shepherd named Plato whose house training was at times questionable.

Hearing his wife Jean in the kitchen, Richard went straight through to admonish her for allowing Plato to go into the spare room, yet as he entered, there was Plato lying on the floor in the kitchen. Richard was stunned. He was adamant that he had just seen Plato enter the spare bedroom, yet Jean was equally adamant that he had never been out of the kitchen.

They checked the room together but there was no sign of a dog, so what had Richard seen? Could it have been the ghost of their beloved German shepherd Gemma, who had died almost a year before? Had she returned in spirit form? She had loved that room and, if she got the chance, had regularly leapt onto the bed and slept for hours. The thought brought back fond memories of Gemma, and although they now had Plato, he would never take her place in their hearts.

During the week Richard was out at work and on one occasion Jean left the house for an hour leaving Plato in the kitchen. On her return she found the kitchen and spare bedroom doors wide open and the bedroom ransacked. She stared in horror at the destruction. The new bedcovers lay in ragged heaps all over the floor, the mattress was torn to shreds and the pillow's contents covered every surface in a jacket of feathers. It could have been the work of some frenzied burglar, yet something was not right. The drawers and cupboards were still closed, nothing had been moved or stolen and there was no evidence of a break-in. Yet wouldn't an opportunist burglar have thought twice about confronting a menacing German shepherd dog on his home territory, and where *was* Plato?

They found him in his basket looking pitifully apologetic and, unbelievably, showing all the signs of being the perpetrator of this destruction. But why? Plato was never aggressive or destructive. What had caused the dog to make such a frenzied attack on the bed? Could the answer be jealousy? Jean and Richard genuinely think it was. They believe that Gemma regularly

Above left and right: Gemma, who regularly comes back in spirit form.

returned in spirit, and did as she enjoyed doing in her lifetime – snoozing on the bed in the spare bedroom. Pluto was obviously aware of this and in a frenzied fight for supremacy with his spirit predecessor, the bed that now showed all the scars, had been their battlefield.

Crystal Torments her Feline Friends

Andrea Sloman is a spiritual healer and although she deals mainly with people, occasionally she also treats animals. One notable animal client was a greyhound called Crystal who suffered from arthritis, yet given the chance she managed to chase Andrea's two cats Indy and Candy around.

After Crystal passed to the spirit world, Andrea noticed that Indy and Candy started to act in a strange way. To put it in Andrea's words, they were acting 'spooked'. The mystery was solved when, at a spiritualist meeting, the serving medium went to Andrea and told her there was a greyhound in her house, chasing her cats. Obviously Crystal had returned in spirit to continue to torment her two feline friends!

The Protective Sitter

It seemed like an easy way to make money, so fifteen-year-old Dawn Barrimore readily agreed to babysit when Mr and Mrs Furness went out for the evening. This became a regular arrangement which suited everyone until Dawn got a boyfriend named Ben and invited him to join her.

One evening Cymba, the family Jack Russell, started acting strangely and Dawn got the distinct impression that he was being protective of her. Ben said to ignore him and drew Dawn towards him in an amorous clinch but, a minute later, Dawn pulled away, listening intently. She had heard a noise upstairs and was sure it was one of the children who had woken up. She went to investigate but found they were both fast asleep.

Cymba, the Jack Russell who sensed the old lady's protective spirit.

When she returned to the sitting room, Cymba was still acting strangely and letting out intermediate low growls, so Ben suggested locking him in the kitchen. Dawn reluctantly agreed and had just settled him in his basket when she heard more noises overhead. They sounded like footsteps and, thinking it was one of the children using the bathroom, Dawn went to check, but found the children were fast asleep and no possible explanation for the noises.

Then Cymba started to whine and howl in a most pitiful way and Dawn was more interested in finding a rational explanation for the noises than Ben's amorous advances. This annoyed Ben who, in a fit of temper, stormed out of the house. Cymba seemed pleased that he had gone and made a big fuss as he was allowed back into the sitting room. They sat watching television together until the doorbell rang. It was Ben, who was having second thoughts.

Dawn was delighted to see him and almost instantly they were in a deep embrace, yet he had changed from being gentle and loving to being very demanding and Dawn wasn't sure she wanted this to go any further. She tried to push him away but he was too strong. She couldn't call out as she didn't want to wake the children and suddenly she realised she was almost powerless to stop him taking advantage of her. Blind panic took hold as she fought desperately to stop him, then suddenly she felt his body go rigid and he shrieked 'What the hell is that?' He leapt up and started backing towards the door. His expression was one of sheer disbelief and panic, his eyes fixed on something at the back of the room. Dawn twisted her head to see the figure of an old lady dressed in dated clothing that seemed to be made of gossamer. Surprisingly, she felt no fear and stared in disbelief as the apparition faded slowly away, then she was jolted out of her trance by the front door slamming loudly. Ben had obviously left in a hurry.

The lonely lane at Abney where a phantom figure led the horse.

Cymba, who had been dancing around barking ecstatically, stopped and stared at the same spot. He also seemed mystified by what he had just witnessed. When the Furness's returned home later they were amazed to hear what had happened. The previous owners of the property had told them about an old lady who apparently appeared in times of need and although they had never seen her, they often had a distinct feeling that someone was watching over them in a protective sort of way. That evening they had been proved right.

The Paralysed Driver

Many years ago, a carter in his horse-drawn trap made a regular journey along the lane from Leadmill to Abney in the Peak District and on various occasions it was claimed that a phantom figure would appear and take the horse's bridle to lead it for a short way. This did not unduly disturb the driver or freak the horse but the driver's dog would cower in the trap, its hair bristling with fear. One day, however, when the phantom appeared, the driver was caught off-guard and involuntarily raised his whip. Instantly his arm fell to his side limp and useless, and he never recovered from his paralysis.

The Ghost in the Graveyard

Gwen and David White and their border collie dog Sammy were walking through Wingerworth graveyard one evening when suddenly a figure swelled up in front of them before disappearing into a yew tree. Sammy, who had been charging around, stopped stock-still with his ears pricked up, staring at the spot.

'Did you see that?' asked David in disbelief.

17

Wingerworth graveyard where David, Gwen and Sammy the border collie saw a ghost.

A carter returning from market was nearly pitched into the River Trent when his horse detected a ghost in the road.

'I did,' said Gwen and was able to describe the phantom as a man wearing black trousers and a white shirt with sleeves rolled up to his elbows although, unnervingly, he was semi-transparent.

Detective Horses

Horses, like dogs and cats, are supersensitive to ghostly activity, as an investigation into the ghostly activity at Spinney Abbey in the heart of the Cambridge fen country showed. Prior to the night's vigil, investigators placed thermometers at various places in order to check for any sudden, inexplicable drop in the night's temperature which might indicate paranormal activity.

Just one thermometer registered an abnormality, a sudden drop of seven degrees at 2.10 a.m. and at the same time horses in the nearby stable suddenly started to make a terrific noise. For several minutes they were kicking their stalls, whinnying and neighing loudly. Gradually they quietened down and by the time the thermometer showed a normal reading at 2.20 a.m., the horses were quiet again.

The Ghost of the Little Chimney Sweep

Fred Buckle was returning home from Newark market. It was getting dark, the cart he was driving had no lights and the path ran alongside the fast-flowing river Trent, but this didn't unduly worry him as Sally, his old grey mare, knew the way home without any help.

The steady, rhythmic trot of her hooves was just lulling him to sleep when Sally suddenly came to an abrupt halt and started to shy away from what Fred thought looked like a pile of soggy wet rags in the middle of the lane. Holding tightly onto the reigns and shouting encouragement to the distressed mare, Fred was suddenly fearful for his own safety. If Sally didn't stop this nonsense, they'd both be pitched into the Trent at any moment.

After what seemed like an age, the mare stopped backing up and Fred shook the reigns to urge her forward again, but she refused point blank. Now feeling rather irritated, he leapt out of the cart and tried to lead her forward, but as she tentatively moved, he noticed she was trembling. It was then that he remembered the pile of wet rags he'd seen in the middle of the lane. Perhaps they were not just rags, but something that had alarmed Sally. He scanned the lane but there was no sign of them. He walked forward cautiously, leading the still-trembling mare, and although they walked some distance, he neither found the pile of rags nor encountered anything extraordinary in the lane.

A few days later, Fred Buckle was recounting this strange incident in his local inn and the landlord said, 'Surely, you've heard about the young chimney sweep who drowned in the river Trent. His pathetic little body was pulled out near there and ever since people have been reporting seeing the ghost of the little chap lying in the middle of the lane.'

The Horse and the Haunted Field

It seemed a perfectly safe place for his young daughter Su to exercise her pony, Dolcy, so when a neighbouring field came up for sale Larry Jackson bought it. Dolcy was brought from the livery stable and installed in her new home, then, watched by her father, twelve-year-old Su saddled her up for their first ride. She started to put Dolcy through her paces but, after the first canter, the pony refused to go down the left-hand side of the field. From whatever direction they approached, Dolcy would do anything to avoid that area, and even after a week she still refused to go into that part of the field.

'It's as if she's afraid of something,' said Su.

'That's nonsense,' said Mr Jackson, and slipping a head collar on Dolcy he led her round the field. All was well until they got almost halfway down the left-hand side where the branches of

Horses are extremely sensitive to the paranormal.

a large tree threw the ground into shadow. Then Dolcy started to pull in the opposite direction and, despite all his efforts, Larry Jackson could not make the pony go into that area.

Some time later, while talking to an elderly farmer who had lived in the village all his life, Larry Jackson told him about the pony's strange behaviour.

'Not surprising,' said the farmer. 'They say that field is haunted and horses can sense that kind of thing. During the Second World War a plane took off from a nearby airfield, but crash landed in that field. The young pilot didn't stand a chance. They say he was flung out on impact and his body was found hanging from a tree halfway down the left-hand side of your field.'

The Traumatised Guard Dogs

RAF Leeming in North Yorkshire has the reputation of being the most haunted airfield in Britain. There have been reports of sudden fiery glows in the centre of the runway, activity in the hangars and unexplainable incidents, but when people outside a hangar saw all the lights come on, then heard the sound of voices inside, they called in security guards. A thorough search revealed nothing, but to ensure airport safety, the security guards locked two of their trained Alsatian guard dogs in the hangar overnight. What those dogs experienced is impossible to know, but in the morning both dogs were so traumatised and unmanageable that they had to be destroyed.

Right: The Little Castle at Bolsover.

Below: Sutton Scarsdale Hall, a romantic ruin that houses many ghosts.

Animals at Historic Properties

Historic properties have their fair share of ghostly visitors. There is one room at Hardwick Old Hall, Derbyshire, where visitors frequently report the feeling of being watched. Others claim to have been touched or spoken to by an invisible person, and both visitors and staff have remarked that this particular room makes them feel uncomfortable.

Dogs do not like this room either. They have been known to go to the far corner and bark at something only they can see or sense. Recently, one of the custodian's dogs stood staring at the far corner of this room with his hackles standing on end. After a short time he gave several low growls then slowly backed out of the room. Was he able to sense some spiritual presence?

Christine, one of the custodians, has probably seen the same thing. She described what she saw as a series of wavy lines outlining one side of a small figure that she believed to be a child. The West Lodge was used as a schoolroom at some point in the past and staff now put any strange experiences down to mischievous ghostly children playing tricks.

At Bolsover Castle, Derbyshire, the three German shepherd dogs of a previous custodian would not enter one particular room on the first floor of the Little Castle previously occupied by a Victorian housekeeper. The dogs, a breed well known for its great courage and heroism, seemed nervous and frightened whenever in that area, yet this is the room where two ex-custodians of the castle chose to stay overnight to raise money for 'Children in Need'. They later reported feeling acutely uneasy, particularly as the dogs with them did not settle all night and paced up and down as if there was the presence of something or someone there with them.

Many visitors to Beeston Castle in Cheshire have reported that their dogs are afraid to go into certain areas. A custodian took a friend's dog with her while she checked the castle but as they approached the West Tower in the inner bailey, the dog stopped, stared straight ahead and began to growl deep in his throat. Despite all her coaxing the dog refused to go any further, unprepared to face what only he could see.

At Calke Abbey on the Derbyshire/Staffordshire border, a normally well-behaved cat was being carried round the house when, according to one of the guides, it suddenly went ballistic. They had just reached the inner hall when the cat sprang out of his arms, raced up the stairs, threw itself at the wall and hurled itself across the landing before charging back down the stairs and outside. Other guides have reported strange phenomena in this area, which was part of the original fabric.

At Brodsworth Hall in Yorkshire, Mary, the housekeeper of the Grant-Dalton family who lived there until 1995, saw several ghostly manifestations. These included an Edwardian gentleman, a chair that rocked on its own and doorknobs that turned by themselves – incidents always accompanied by manic barking and rushing round by the family dogs.

Woburn Abbey, the Bedfordshire seat of the Dukes of Bedford, is built on the site of a Cistercian abbey and houses many ghosts that apparently the dogs do not like. Often they will stop suddenly in one of the long corridors, crouch down with their tails between their legs, howl piteously and refuse to move.

Sutton Scarsdale Hall is a romantic ruin that a century ago was the inspiration for D.H. Lawrence's *Lady Chatterley's Lover*. Stripped of its roof and anything of value in the 1920s, the building's gradual decay was halted by English Heritage who acquired the property a decade ago and sent in a team of workmen to make the structure safe. During this time, the basement was used as a store and workshop, and was the only area that was heated.

One bitterly cold day the workmen took pity on one of the cats that roamed the area and carried it down into the warmth, but almost immediately the cat arched its back and started to spit and hiss at one area of the basement room. The workmen could see nothing, but the cat obviously could and after this show of aggression it shot up the stairs and out of the building. Various ghost-hunting groups have staked out Sutton Scarsdale Hall and all have reported ghostly happenings, including the appearance of a grey lady and a dismembered hand beckoning from the basement staircase.

Many years ago it was believed that a haunted tunnel linked Walsingham Abbey with Binham Priory in Norfolk. One day a travelling fiddler boasted to local people that he was not afraid to go through the haunted tunnel and so, accompanied by his faithful little dog, he set off, playing his fiddle as he went so that the villagers could track his progress from above the ground.

All was well until he reached a hill, then the music stopped. The villagers waited, expecting to hear the fiddler again on the far side of the hill, but there was only silence. Suddenly, the little dog streaked out of the tunnel entrance, obviously terrified, but the fiddler was never seen again. The mount became known as Fiddler's Hill until in 1933 road widening work cut into the hill and it was realised that it was in fact an ancient barrow where three skeletons, including one of a dog, were found.

Brunel's Great Western Railway buildings in Swindon are now English Heritage offices yet they seem to have retained a ghost from those earlier days, a ghost that dogs can detect as soon as they enter the building. In fact, most dogs are reluctant to go through the main entrance of the building or the passage beyond it. Even the large, fierce dogs used by security firms pull away and refuse to go anywhere near a certain area where, one night in the early 1990s, a security guard patrolling with his dog heard the sound of a clock being wound. He went to investigate and sure enough, standing facing a wall with his back to him, stood a man clearly operating a winding key, yet there was no sign of a clock. The security guard challenged him and the man turned to reveal that he had no face.

Not surprisingly, the security guard and his dog were so disturbed by this incident that the guard was hospitalised and the poor dog had to be put down.

Later investigations showed that during the time when the building was used as railway offices, there had in fact been a clock on the wall the apparition had faced, and it needed regular winding with a key.

The Guard Dog that Turned White with Fright

Nottingham Castle (of Robin Hood fame) is now a museum and regularly patrolled by security guards. There is also an alarm system that is linked to the police, so recently when the alarms went off, the security guard on duty simply walked down to the gatehouse and waited for their arrival. Very soon, along came a police vehicle with two officers and the biggest, most ferocious-looking black and tan German shepherd dog.

They all walked up to the castle and made a thorough search, yet found nothing. Then suddenly the temperature started to plummet for no explainable reason, and the men felt uneasy. The hair on the back of their necks prickled with fear, and the dog was obviously experiencing something too. His hackles rose, he snarled and growled, and pulled so hard to get at something unseen by the men that his handler had great difficulty holding him back. The dog's unaccountable behaviour did very little to reassure the men, who all left hurriedly, pulling the snarling dog with them.

Several days later, one of the policemen called to see the security guard who at the time was on duty in the castle gatehouse. Apparently none of the men who had been present that night could account for what had happened, but the dog had spent the night whimpering plaintively. The following morning his handler had found him cowering in the corner of his pen and his fur had turned white with fright.

II

DO ANIMALS KNOW WHEN DEATH IS IMMINENT?

There's a rural belief in the New Forest that when the reigning sovereign is going to die a huge red deer stag haunts the King's Tree, the one that purportedly deflected the arrow that killed King William Rufus. Because William was known as the Red King, the stag has been named the Red King's Deer. Verderers say the size of its slots (footprints) show how heavy it is and how fast it is going; if it stands a while, the death wouldn't be for a nearly a year, but if it is galloping the death is imminent.

The slots were apparently seen by forest keepers in 1820 when King George III died, in 1830 prior to the death of George IV and in 1836 on the death of George V. It was seen when Queen Victoria died in 1901, prior to the death of Edward VII in 1910, George V in 1936 and when King George VI died in 1952.

In Ireland, they believe that if a strange dog starts digging in the garden, it's a sure sign that illness or death will follow. To hear the howl of a dog is also said to be a forewarning of death as later stories will show, and in rural England ferrets and weasels too were thought to be creatures of ill-omen, bringing death or disaster by their presence or call. These might only be old superstitions, yet it is a known fact that animals are able to predict illness and some pets seem able to predict the death of their owners. Many even start to pine before that person has actually died.

A scientific explanation would be that animals can sense the chemical changes that the human body undergoes when close to death. Animals may also pick up the weak electrical field around a human, generated by the electricity in the body's nerves and muscles, but could there be some other power at work? Dogs have been known to howl when there is a death in the family even if that person is hundreds of miles away, and before the message has been received, so how does a dog detect the death of his master when he is far away?

Just before President Abraham Lincoln was assassinated, his dog is said to have howled and run around the White House in great distress.

When the famous Egyptologist Lord Carnarvon funded Howard Carter to discover the secrets of Tutankhamen's tomb, it is said that the mummy put a curse on him. This was probably a story invented by a journalist, yet two months later on 6 April 1923, Lord Carnarvon died in Cairo. When the news was received in England, relatives were able to confirm that at exactly the time of his death, his faithful dog started howling plaintively and died within a few hours.

Above left: How did President Lincoln's dog know his master was about to die?

Above right: Duke was waiting to die with his master.

Together Forever

Ted Wells spent his last few days in hospital while his faithful old dog Duke was being cared for by his son. The nursing staff knew that Ted's time was near, so they were extremely surprised when suddenly he sat up in bed and called out 'Come on Duke, let's go for a walk!'. Then he slumped back onto the bed and died.

At his son's house at exactly the same time, Duke let out a wild, almost ecstatic bark, lay down and promptly died.

Best Friends

When friends Amy and Babs were looking for puppies they chose two brothers from the same litter and, as the pups grew, the two dogs remained the best of friends. One evening Amy's dog Jude suddenly let out two terrifying yelps then slunk into his basket. Jude was obviously in some dreadful pain and Amy was understandably alarmed, yet despite checking him over, she could find no reason for the cries.

After keeping a close eye on him for ten minutes, by which time he was sleeping quite peacefully, she decided to ring her friend Babs for a bit of reassurance.

Bab's husband answered the phone and from his voice Amy could tell he was very upset. The reason – fifteen minutes earlier, at exactly the same time that Jude had cried so scarily, their dog had been involved in an accident and been killed.

Litter mates are able to sense when the other is not well.

Messengers of the Dead

Birds, both domestic and wild are believed to be able to foretell death. A cockerel crowing uncharacteristically in the hours of darkness was thought to mean the approach of death somewhere in the vicinity. Hens showing signs of fear or panic in spite of the absence of any predator in the area were often believed to be foretelling doom for someone close by. If a raven flew in front of a person, it was believed to be a bad sign – death was not far away. Birds tapping on the window of a house were an equally unfortunate sign, as was a seagull standing on one leg on the roof of a house.

Birds were at one time believed to be the messengers of the dead. Sparrows, larks and storks were said to carry the souls of people from the Guff (Hall of Souls) in Heaven, to earth. Other birds, especially crows, were believed to carry the spirits of humans on to the next plain of existence.

The Pigeons Knew

Graham Wildgoose had always been a keen pigeon fancier, but in his latter years he was forced to live in a city apartment where pets were not allowed. This did not unduly worry Graham because every day at the same time, a flock of pigeons, many that he knew by name, arrived at his apartment block and Graham went out to feed 'his birds'. When he was taken ill suddenly and confined to bed, the pigeons still returned every day and sat quietly, many with their heads under their wings, waiting patiently. As Graham passed into spirit, as if in response to some bizarre sign, they all took flight and never returned. They knew that Graham would never feed them again.

Above: Gordon, Adrian, Dena, Sophia and Elf in the Lake District.

Left: Birds are believed to be able to foretell death.

Elf

Animals seem also to know when to expect their *own* death. Whenever we went out, our keeshond Elf was always ready and eager to come with us on a car journey, but not this particular time. He simply lay in the garden and looked at me as I tried to coax him. When it was obvious that he didn't want to come, I tried to make him go into the house until we returned, but he refused, so we left him in the garden. When we returned a few hours later, he was dead and he had never moved.

Flint

We brought Flint from the animal rescue centre and shared four, memorable years with him, but tragically, he gradually developed paralysis in his hind legs.

Despite all the efforts of the vet and ludicrously expensive treatment, Flint wasn't improving. He hadn't been active for some time and just seemed to want to lie down. He started spending his days in a shady spot in the garden, then when he refused to come in one evening, I feared the worst. Despite the temptation of warm blankets and a cosy bed he wanted to stay outside and during the night I was woken by Flint howling plaintively. That was just before he died.

Astral Barks

The Bradley family's chihuahua had been outside rather a long time. It was December and the weather was freezing, so they went outside to search without success. Back in the house Dorothy Bradley heard him give a series of shrill barks, his usual reaction to anything unfamiliar, and they went back outside with a torch. They found his little body – he had been dead for at

Above: Flint, our gentle giant.

Right: Micky, the little white West Highland terrier.

least twenty minutes — so how did the dead chihuahua give those astral barks to tell the family where he was?

Micky Says Goodbye

This is a story that was first told in the *London Daily News* in 1920. A man was travelling by train across Europe to a new job in Romania when a young woman entered his carriage. She asked in rather shaky English if the little white dog was with him. He looked around but saw no sign of a dog, so assuming she had made a translation error, he smiled and nodded. After a while he fell asleep and woke to hear persistent scratching. For a second he was back home in England and his little white West Highland Terrier Micky was scratching at the door. The man looked around the carriage and although he could find no reason for the noise, he felt rather agitated.

When he arrived in Romania, he wrote a long letter to his wife, mentioned these strange incidents, and asked how Micky was. His wife then broke the news that Micky had been run over. The time coincided with the time the young woman had seen 'the little white dog' in the railway carriage, and at the exact time he had heard what he thought was Micky scratching, the little dog lay dying in the arms of his mistress hundreds of miles away.

There are occasions when a duplicate of a person or an animal still alive or on the point of death, appears as a ghost-double. They act quite normally and it is only later that these doubles are found to be in two different places at the same time. They are given the German name Doppelganger and their appearance is taken as an ominous sign, forewarning death.

The Doppelganger Cat

When author T.C. Lethbridge's eighteen-year-old cat developed a mouth infection in October 1966, Mrs Lethbridge took it to the vet.

At the same time, Mr Lethbridge had a visitor who asked, 'Is this the cat you write about in your books?'

Mr Lethbridge looked up to see the cat standing on the fireside stool, apparently smelling the visitor's hand. He confirmed that it was the cat, completely forgetting that his wife had actually taken their cat to the vet.

Shortly afterwards, Mrs Lethbridge arrived home minus the cat, who had been left with the vet to have a tooth extracted under anaesthetic. Sadly, the cat died and it was then that Lethbridge realised that the cat had been in two locations – at the vet's and on the stool – at the same time. The double of this cat had somehow managed to project itself back to its comfortable home.

Bruce, the Doppelganger Dog

Their marriage had ended quite amicably, but for Monica the hardest part was leaving her beloved dog Bruce behind with her husband. It wasn't a decision she had taken lightly but as she was making a new life for herself in the Isle of Wight, it seemed cruel to uproot the old dog.

During those first few weeks, she missed Bruce terribly, particularly when she walked through the leafy lanes. Then one day, as she walked alone, she was suddenly joined by Bruce. Her initial shock was replaced by delight as she ran towards the dog and threw her arms round him, but her arms passed straight through him. Shocked and distressed, she phoned her husband who informed her that Bruce had died that morning at the same time that he had appeared to Monica.

The Spirit Escort

This touching story is rather different because it was a spirit pet that came back to warn her owners that her successor was about to die.

When Jean and Richard Low's beloved Emer (an Irish name pronounced Eema) died they bought Gemma, who grew to be almost the spiting image of Emer with the same silver markings in her black coat.

Jean was recovering from a gallstone operation and spent many hours in bed with Gemma curled up beside her, so in the evenings, rather than disturb her, Richard would make himself comfortable on the settee, watch television and invariably after a hard day's work, fall asleep.

He awoke one evening to find himself looking directly into the eyes of a German shepherd dog who immediately turned and walked out of the room. He heard her bound upstairs and enter their bedroom, so pulling himself up, he followed and found, as he had expected, Jean snoozing on the bed with Gemma beside her.

'Gemma has just been downstairs with me,' Richard informed Jean who looked at him in surprise, then shook her head.

'She can't have been. She's never moved from my side,' said Jean.

They looked at each other in disbelief. Richard was adamant he had seen Gemma downstairs, yet Jean was equally adamant that Gemma had never left the bedroom.

It was then that Jean realised that it hadn't been Gemma at all. The dog that Richard had seen was Emer and now it was Jean's turn to be upset. They firmly believed that Emer had returned to draw their attention to the fact that Gemma was ill, and their worst fears were confirmed when they subsequently took her to the vet who diagnosed cancer. Despite all the efforts of the vet and their reluctance to let her go, they had to accept the inevitable and allow the vet to administer the fatal dose. The one positive thing that made the parting bearable was knowing that their two beloved dogs would be together in the spirit world.

Above left: Richard with Emer.

Above right: Gemma, whose predecessor Emer came back to warn Jean and Richard that Gemma was dying.

It's not easy to let a beloved pet go, but this poem might help to make it a little easier.

Someday I'll grow frail and weak
And pain may keep me from my sleep
Then you must do what must be done
For this last battle can't be won

You will be sad – I understand
Don't let your grief then stay your hand
For this day, more than all the rest
Your love and friendship stand the test

We've had so many happy years
What is to come can hold no fears

You'd not want me to suffer so
When the time comes, please let me go

Take me where my needs they'll tend
It is a kindness you do for me my friend
Although my tale its last has waved
From pain and suffering I've been saved

Don't grieve that it should be you
Who must decide this thing to do
We've been so close for many years
Don't let your heart hold any tears.

III

THEIR LAST GOODBYES

If there is life after death, why not for our pets? Does the bond that we have transcend the grave? Many owners believe that it does. Glenda told me that she saw the shape of her beloved dog Sandy through their smoked-glass front door panel although he had been dead for weeks. After David's Weimaraner died, he often heard the clicking of his dog's long nails on the sitting room's wooden floor. Sylvia and her husband saw the kitchen door open the way their cat Whisk always nudged it, but Whisk was no longer with them. There was no breeze or draft or reason to cause the door to open and they were both convinced it was Whisk in astral form, letting them know he was still around.

These are not just isolated incidents as this chapter shows.

Matty's Experience

All pet owners dread the day when their animals are old and ill and the kindest thing they can do is let the vet administer that fatal dose. It is a terrible experience. When this happened to Matty's dog Siba, she covered her in a blanket and, as it was late, she arranged for her son to dig a hole in the garden to bury Siba the following day. As Matty went up to bed that night she lovingly touched Siba's collar and lead that hung on the hall stand, but couldn't bring herself to remove it, not yet. She cried herself to sleep, but it was a very troubled sleep.

Suddenly she was wide awake and listening to the constant rattling of Siba's collar and lead. Siba had always taken hold of it in her teeth and rattled it like that as a sign that she wanted to be taken for a walk. Matty charged downstairs expecting to see her beloved pet, but the hall was empty and the collar and lead hung silently on the hall stand.

Boy

When Ray Neil's dog Boy died, he felt as though he had lost his dearest friend. Life seemed very empty, and not being ready to get another dog, he often took his parent's dog Mat for walks along the same paths he had walked with Boy. In fact, he had regularly taken both dogs as they had always been firm friends.

It was late one evening as Ray and Mat walked along by the river when suddenly Mat began to wag his tail and pull excitedly on his lead. It was obvious from his behaviour that he had seen something that had animated him, but what, Ray couldn't tell in the dim light.

Then Ray saw the waiting figure. It was a dog and from Mat's reaction a friend, so he released the spring on the extendable lead and Mat ran excitedly forward. Ray saw the two dogs meet, then he stopped dead in his tracks. The other dog was Boy – it couldn't be any other with those

Left: Pets will often come back in spirit form to say goodbye.

Below: Kirsche.

markings. Ray started to run forward but as he did so, Boy seemed to be pulled away from them by some unseen power. It had all happened so quickly and as he reached down to pat Mat, he realised that he too was hugely perplexed by what he had just witnessed. Although still in shock, Mat's reaction helped Ray come to terms with Boy's appearance to say a final goodbye to his two best friends.

Kirsche

Jacqui's four dogs lived in a luxury kennel block in the garden, yet on 20 June 2005, Kirsche, her keeshond bitch, spent the whole day following Jacqui around the house. From this unusual behaviour Jacqui knew something was wrong and the next day this was confirmed by the vet who put Kirsche to sleep. She was buried in the garden, but a week later when Jacqui was standing at the kitchen surface preparing food, she knew Kirsche had returned when she felt her cold nose sniff her leg in the inimitable way she had always begged for food.

Jacqui looked down but there was no sign of Kirsche and the other three dogs were in the garden.

Flint

Flint, our Labrador dog, had died just days before Kirsche, and after telling me about Kirshe's return, Jacqui asked if Flint had been back. I said he hadn't and thought no more about it until my daughter Sophia, now living in London, came home for a visit.

Flint had always been Sophia's dog. It was Sophia and I who went to choose him from the Northern Labrador Rescue Society; it was Sophia who socialised him, played with him and walked him regularly before she left home. Because of his mobility problem, we used to leave Flint in the kitchen if we were going upstairs, and he would flop behind the kitchen door, listening and waiting for our return. Towards the end of his life, he had slowed down and had great difficulty moving his seven-and-a-half-stone bulk in time to avoid being pushed by the opening door. As the door would not open until he had moved, we regularly had to stand in the hall waiting.

Sophia hadn't been there during his last illness or at the time of his death, and this was her first visit since. She had only been home a few hours when she tried to push open the kitchen door and found that it was obstructed. Momentarily forgetting that Flint was no longer with us, she instinctively waited and listened for him to pull himself up and amble away, then pushed the door again. This time there was no resistance, but neither was there any sign of Flint. We think he was waiting for Sophia to return so that he could say his last goodbye.

But that's not all. When I returned home last week, I parked my car in the drive as my husband let our three shih-tzus out of the house. They ran across the garden in their usual enthusiastic way, leaping and barking ecstatically, but over the sound of their shrill barks, I heard a distinctive gruff bark. It was low, familiar and instantly recognisable as Flint. It is sad but reassuring to think that although we can't see him, he's still around watching what we are doing.

I was relating this to the staff at my local library when a lady approached me.

'I hope you don't think I was eavesdropping,' she said apologetically, 'but I've had similar experiences. I've had three cats and each one has come back to say goodbye.'

Grantchester

Stella's first cat was named Grantchester. He died at the age of thirteen and Stella was understandably heartbroken. Then one night, she was in bed fast asleep when she felt something snuggling up against her the way Grantchester always had.

Flint.

'Is that you Grantchester?' Stella whispered in disbelief and Grantchester instantly replied with a 'Brrrrrrr…'

Suddenly Stella was wide awake and reached down to stroke Grantchester, but there was nothing there. Stella tried to convince herself it was a dream, until it happened again the next night then every night for the next two months. Her beloved pet had returned as a ghost and they shared the same intimate little conversations, but towards the end Grantchester kept telling Stella to get another cat. Once Stella agreed to do this, Grantchester never returned.

Kango

Pearl Warner lived in an old cottage next door to a farm in Yorkshire. To help keep down the mice, she always had a cat and in the late 1970s Pearl had a ginger tom called Kango brought from the RSPCA. Kango was a delightful character and a constant companion but he had no interest in mousing. In the five years Pearl had him, he never caught a thing! After his death, Pearl got another cat and this time it was a great mouser, preferring to spend its time in the neighbouring barns rather than with Pearl. She should have been pleased, but she missed the companionship of Kango Then one night she had just gone to bed and turned off the light when she felt a cat jump up onto the bed and curl up the way Kango had always done. She switched on the light but could see nothing, the bedroom door was closed and her cat was not even in the house.

Putting it down to imagination, she returned to bed but, as she lay there, she felt the ghost cat return. He walked over her feet to find a comfortable position then paddled the bed with its paws exactly as Kango had always done. Having made himself comfortable, she heard him purr and even felt the vibrations as he sat washing himself. Pearl was convinced it was Kango who had returned.

Fuggly

Jacqui Cooke had a cat called Fuggly who was very vociferous. He would wander round the house meowing constantly as if having a deep and meaningful conversation. One day he was unfortunately run over, but shortly afterwards, Jacqui began hearing him again. She knew it was Fuggly because the meowing was exactly like the usual conversation he had always had. However Jacqui wasn't just able to *hear* Fuggly, she also saw him flit across rooms and pass open doorways.

Smokey

It was a weekend in late October and the clocks had been moved back, so in order to go to bed at her usual time of 10.30 p.m. it was actually an hour later when Sarah went to bed on the Sunday night. The glow from the outside light illuminated the room, but as she walked round the bed she almost fell over something on the carpeted floor. She stared in disbelief because there sat her cat Smokey.

But that was impossible; Smokey had been dead almost a year, but his look undeniably said 'where have you been then?' before he promptly disappeared.

Was it Bumble or Sproggy Dog?

Gwen White has owned dogs and cats for many years and in a quiet corner of her Wingerworth home under the shade of a cherry tree, she has a small cemetery for all her past pets. While on her knees tending this one day, she felt an animal brush along the base of her back and, thinking it was Bumble, her Persian cat who spent most of his time in the house, she said, 'Hey Bumble, what are you doing out here?'

As she spoke, Gwen turned but found she was completely alone. She checked in the house and found Bumble fast asleep; so what had she felt?

Gwen was mystified, yet people she told about this said it must have been a freak gust of wind – what other explanation could they offer? But Gwen knew it was not wind and became more and more convinced that it was Sproggy Dog, her former scrubbing-brush-look-alike pet, who had come back to say he was all right.

Gwen had never forgiven herself for not being there when Sproggy Dog died. She had woken at 3.00 a.m. one morning hearing her pet screaming in agony and, being unable to do anything for him, phoned her niece Joanne, a veterinary nurse. It was Joanne who was with Sproggy Dog at the end, so was this his way of returning to say goodbye to his grieving mistress?

Twinkle

There are numerous stories of human ghosts being reflected in mirrors, ghosts that are otherwise not visible. Here is a similar phenomenon of a ghost cat.

Wendy Grosset was heartbroken when her cat Twinkle died. Her apartment felt strangely empty and after a troubled night she left early to drive to work in one of Newcastle's modern office blocks. She let herself in and walked towards the full-length, glass doors at the far end of reception. She could see her own reflection in the glass and, walking beside her with his tail held high, was Twinkle. She looked down immediately but she couldn't see or feel anything. Looking back towards the doors again, not only was her own reflection clearly visible, but so was Twinkle's, yet as she approached the doors, her beloved cat disappeared.

Cats regularly return to say goodbye to
their grieving owners. *Clockwise from top left:*
Grantchester; Fuggly; Cindy, Smokey; Twinkle.

Mickey

Mr and Mrs Leonard were sitting reading in their sitting room one evening. Their Pekingese dog, Ching, was sleeping on the floor, but their cat Mickey, who would normally have been there too, had died three weeks previously. Mrs Leonard looked up from her book and gasped in amazement because the astral body of Mickey was sitting on a shelf beneath a table. Almost at the same moment Ching began barking furiously; her eyes were bulging and her cheeks puffing in and out with excitement as she rushed towards Mickey. The astral cat, however, did exactly as he had done when he was alive, and leapt up onto a side table out of Ching's reach. There he sat, looking down at the excited Pekingese who was jumping up and down trying to get to him.

Mrs Leonard petted Mickey, and Ching barked furiously all the time, but Mr Leonard couldn't understand what all the fuss was about as he could not see Mickey at all.

Bess

Simon Burrows ran an isolated farm in the Yorkshire Dales, but as he was due to retire he had reduced his flock of sheep to a more manageable size for himself and his faithful sheepdog Bess. Then Bess died suddenly and Simon decided he didn't want the hassle of training another dog for the short time he had left. He decided he could manage alone, but one dark winter's night Simon found the task almost impossible and, in exasperation, he let out an almost inaudible whistle. Suddenly the form of Bess appeared and rounded up the flock while Simon stood in total, bewildered silence. As he went to lock the pen with the sheep safely inside, the ghost of Bess simply melted away.

Buster

One winter night not long after Buster, her golden retriever, had died, Jean returned home after walking her other retriever Basil. It was a horrible, rainy night and they were both soaked, so she left Basil in the kitchen while she ran upstairs to get towels and a hairdryer.

A few minutes later she returned and as she passed, glanced through the open door into the sitting room. Pushing open the kitchen door, realisation hit: she had just seen a dog lying on the rug in the sitting room. Obviously her husband must have let Basil out of the kitchen, yet that was not possible – he was still there in the kitchen looking wet and bedraggled.

She returned hurriedly to the sitting room, but it was now empty and it was only then that she realised the dog she had seen was dry and clean and the only explanation was that Buster had returned in spirit.

Poppy

Mandy Jenner felt the loss of her cat Poppy very deeply. She had always been a playful cat although at times she was quite a nuisance, particularly when Mandy was knitting. Mandy would try to conceal the ball of wool, but Poppy always managed to release it, chase it round the floor and box it playfully with her paw before tossing it in the air. This had become a regular game.

A short time after Poppy's death, Mandy resumed her knitting and, as the knitting needles clicked away, the ball of wool fell to the floor where she left it. Without Poppy, there was no urgency, her beloved cat was no longer there to play. Then suddenly the ball moved in a quick jerk as if knocked by an invisible paw. No sooner had it stopped than it moved again and this time rolled a little bit further. Mandy stared in amazement. The first time, she might have inadvertently pulled the wool, but not the second time. She told herself she was imagining

Left: Ghosts of deceased animals rarely appear in photographs like this 1925 snapshot. The boy is holding a pet rabbit, yet next to it on the right is the ghost of a white kitten, identified as a family pet previously mauled by a dog.

Below: The lonely dales where Bess helped her master herd the sheep.

Above left: Golden Labrador retrievers.

Above right: Truss, the Old English sheepdog.

things and continued with her knitting, but as she paused the same thing happened again and this time there was no doubt in Mandy's mind. Although she was invisible to her, Mandy was sure that Poppy was there enjoying her usual game.

Just Checking

Shortly after Truss, their Old English Sheepdog, died, the Black family chose a rescue dog from the local centre. Of mixed parentage, he obviously had some greyhound in him as he made a habit of racing as fast as he could round the huge lawn at the back of their house. For this reason, they called him Swift.

He settled well, but one day Swift was at the bottom of the garden and even at that distance, from his body movements, Ted Black could see that he was particularly excited about something. When he made a series of strange, unfamiliar yelps, Ted decided to investigate, thinking he'd caught a rabbit or a hedgehog or something.

Ted found him looking into the corner of the garden where old Truss had been buried, and there as plain as day, taking a very interested look at this latest edition to the family, was Truss. Ted blinked and looked back, but in that instant Truss had gone.

Animal ghosts are sometimes visible to other people yet their owners can't see them, as these next stories show.

Kalle

Liz and her husband regularly drove to a nearby pub for Sunday lunch. Their dog Kalle always accompanied them and, while they ate, he snoozed in the car. If they were longer than an hour, Kalle got bored and would jump into the driver's seat where he would sit looking out the window. He had also learnt that by pressing on a lever, he could flash the lights on and off, and this became his party piece.

It was a few weeks after Kalle's death that Liz and her husband visited the pub again and, as they were leaving, the head waiter gave them their usual doggy bag. They thanked him but said

Chalky the white cat.

sadly it wasn't necessary as Kalle had unfortunately died. The waiter stared in stunned disbelief. He said he had just been looking out of the kitchen window and had seen the car lights flashing on and off and he had waved as he always did to Kalle who was sitting looking out of the driver's window.

Chalky

Paul Vest noticed a large angora cat dozing in the sun on his neighbour's porch. He wasn't aware until then that they had a cat and as he watched, the cat got up lazily, stretched and ambled off. He noticed that despite its thick white coat, it had strange black markings on its hind legs. Later he mentioned the cat to Madge, his neighbour, who passed it off as a neighbourhood stray until he mentioned the strange black markings.

Madge visibly blanched. 'That was Chalky,' she said, staring at Paul incredulously. 'But it couldn't be. Chalky was killed months ago.'

She insisted on going outside and searching the garden but there was no sign of the cat. Then she showed Paul photographs of Chalky. If that mystery cat hadn't been Chalky it was certainly his identical twin.

Paul had forgotten the incident until one day he glanced over into his neighbour's garden and saw two cats playing in the grass. He stopped in his tracks and stared in disbelief. One cat was a brown tabby, but the other was the white cat, the one Madge had believed to be Chalky. He watched the two cats for a moment, then ran over to the fence to get a better view. Startled, the white cat turned and stared at him – then suddenly – it was no longer there. Only the brown tabby remained, apparently shadow-boxing with itself. He stood staring at the brown cat as it continued to play with an invisible companion. It was obvious from the action of the brown cat that Chalky continued playing too but Paul could no longer see him.

Paul could find no explanation apart from − fantastic as it seemed − he had seen the ghost of Chalky − a cat killed months before. But if that was so, Chalky was living in some invisible dimension within the boundaries of his former home. Also, it seemed evident that the brown cat could see Chalky and play with him as though Chalky was still there in his physical body.

The whole experience puzzled Paul to such an extent that he persuaded a friend to bring his black cat over to observe her reaction to the ghost cat who lived next door. They took the black cat into Madge's garden and put her down. She picked her way disinterestedly about, and nothing unusual happened until she started to go onto the porch. Suddenly she froze on the steps, hissing and baring her fangs. She was staring wide-eyed at the identical spot on the porch where Paul had first seen the white cat dozing in the sun.

'Do you think she sees Chalky?' Madge enquired nervously.

'She certainly sees something,' Paul replied as they all stared at the strange antics of the black cat, 'but they don't seem to be kindred spirits.'

Hissing and spitting, the black cat suddenly turned and bolted.

'That's so strange,' said Madge. 'Chalky never could stand black cats.'

Gem Takes a Ride

Sue was waiting at the bus stop when Cassy, an acquaintance from the village, pulled her car up alongside and offered her a lift. As it was bitterly cold, Sue was grateful but as she pulled open the passenger door, she noticed the dog in the centre of the back seat. She was rather nervous around dogs, but this one seemed docile and had made no move towards her, so she jumped in and pulled the door closed. As Cassy pulled away, Sue located the seat belt and half turned to find the connection point. As she did so, she glanced into the back of the car but the seat was empty. She did a double take. What had happened to the dog? She twisted round to look on the floor, but that was empty too.

'Are you okay?' asked Cassy, rather bewildered by her passenger's strange twisting and turning.

Sue looked puzzled. 'The dog?' she said. 'Where is it?'

Gem, the border terrier that still enjoyed riding in the car.

Some spirit pets come back to say goodbye.

Cassy was silent for a few seconds. 'There is no dog,' she said, her voice cracking with emotion.

'But I definitely saw a dog,' insisted Sue. 'A small, short coated, shaggy dog was sitting in the middle of that seat when I got into this car. I saw it as plain as I can see you.'

'That's impossible,' vowed Cassy on the verge of tears. The description fitted Gem, her border terrier with her harsh, grizzle coat, but Gem had died three months previously. Gem had always accompanied Cassy whenever she went out in the car and her favourite spot was the centre of the back seat.

Once she had got over the initial shock of Sue seeing Gem, it gave Cassy tremendous satisfaction to think that Gem still accompanied her in the car.

Bonnie and Cara

Derek Acorah, the spiritual medium, dedicated his book *The Psychic Adventures of Derek Acorah* to the memory of his beloved dogs Cara and Bonnie. Despite being a renowned medium, Derek is highly sensitive and still experiences the feelings of grief and loss like we all do when a beloved person or pet passes from our physical world and on to the world of spirit.

In the book he expresses his sorrow at losing his seventeen-year-old German shepherd, Cara, yet informs us that he has seen Cara around his home on many occasions since that sad day. She returns to sit in her favourite places and occasionally he will hear her bark. Clairvoyantly, he has also seen her bound joyously across the fields, young once more and not burdened by the ravages of age.

IV

MAKING CONTACT WITH YOUR SPIRIT PET

Seeing or sensing your pet in spirit is often dismissed as a figment of the imagination, a vision or even a dream. A number of pet owners seem embarrassed to admit such things happen, yet for many it is a valuable part of the grieving process, an experience they find comforting and beneficial.

Communicating with your departed pets, particularly if the parting was sudden or tragic, gives owners an opportunity to tell their pet how much they meant to them and how much they miss them.

As the previous stories show, some people momentarily sense, see or feel a beloved pet. At the same time, other animals present may stare intently at one particular spot and bark furiously, wag their tails or purr. They are no doubt able to see or sense them too. After passing to spirit, animals can decide, just as humans can, whether or not they wish to return to their old surroundings and the place where they have been loved.

We all know how hard it is to say goodbye, we grieve for the physical presence of our pets, and some people would rather not see their pet after its death as they feel it might upset them and increase their sense of loss. In that case, they will not have the experience, because their pet would not wish to distress them further.

On the other hand, if you want your pet to return, you need to ask it to do so. Open yourself up to spirit influences by being sensitive and intuitive. Speak to your pet telepathically. Tell him about your cherished memories of all the times you've spent together, the funny times and the sad. It's highly unlikely that anything will happen immediately but have faith and patience, and be prepared. It is the unexpectedness that is often frightening, and it is normal to get upset, but take several deep breaths to slow down your heart rate, and try to relax. Most sightings are over in less than sixty seconds.

I can't guarantee that you will see or sense your pet but if you want to induce such experiences, the following suggestions may help you.

Take an object that belonged to your pet. This could be a blanket, toy, bowl, collar and lead, harness or jacket. Hold it carefully, as the item will have absorbed the energies of your pet and his key personality is somehow etched on these familiar items. It is possible to pick up on these energies, activated by the power of positive thought. This is called psychometrizing, and with a little concentration, anyone who is sensitive can tune into the vibrations of the object and be inspired with comforting thoughts.

Belongings will have absorbed your pet's energy.

Follow your normal lifestyle and the pattern that will be familiar to your pet. If possible, go to the grave or a favourite spot in the garden. Use all your senses. Speak to your pet telepathically, murmuring the words of endearment that you used with your pet when you were alone. Picture him, listen for his bark or purr, and for a second, you may hear your animal's snuffle in your mind. Remember the texture of his coat and his smell. This will often evoke strong memories.

Before sleep, think about your pet. Tell your pet how much you loved him and how your life has been enriched by the times you spent together. When you close your eyes, picture your pet in your mind's eye and it is highly possible that you will dream of the pet you have lost.

Spiritual Experiences

If you have never been to a spiritual church, perhaps now is the time to pay a visit. Most spiritual churches have a Sunday service plus a healing service and a psychic service during the week, so check this out. Don't go along feeling that something is definitely going to happen. Keep an open mind and be prepared to be amazed.

Jean and Richard Low are Christian spiritualists who regularly attend their local spiritual church and apparently so too does their golden retriever Blondie, although she has been dead many years. Visiting spiritual leaders at their church regularly report seeing a golden dog from the spirit world hovering beside them. Jean has also been told by visiting mediums that her childhood pet Penny, a wirehaired cross-breed, is also often seen by her side.

The author with her arms full of beautiful puppies. One of these adorable bundles was Beau, who died in July 2002 aged fourteen.

Beau's grave in the garden.

Above: Blondie is a regular visitor at the spiritual church where her owners worship.

Left: Beau driving his cosi pet car.

Andrea Sloman was once asked to give spiritual healing to a racing pigeon and some time later, while attending her spiritual church, a medium reported seeing a pigeon in spirit form with her.

Andrea's two cats Candy and Indy passed to spirit in 2005 and since then they have both been seen by medium friends. Candy was witnessed frolicking amongst bluebells and Indy sitting on Andrea's lap. Andrea has also seen Indy's ginger fur in her inner vision.

I contacted Edith Farrow, a trusted psychic medium who has been practising for over thirty years. Because she is very strict about client confidentiality, she was unwilling to divulge any names, but informed me that many people who visit her for a consultation walk in, unbeknown to them, accompanied by their spirit pets. People seem unable to accept this as a fact until she gives them the name of their departed pet. Usually it is a dog or a cat, and it happens so regularly that Edith refers to them as fur babies.

There are however several notable exceptions. About four years ago, a teenager went to Edith for a consultation and she was amazed to see a horse looking over the girl's shoulder. It was a first for Edith to see a spirit horse, and when she mentioned this, the girl broke down in tears. It was the girl's horse and it had been put down the previous week.

A man went for a consultation and Edith immediately picked up on a greyhound that followed him into the room. As he sat down, the greyhound lay down at his feet and Edith noticed the bandage on one of its paws.

'You have a dog lying at your feet,' she told the man. 'It's a greyhound and it has a bandage round one paw.'

The man was very upset. It had been his greyhound that for some reason had started biting his paw and continued until he was actually eating it away. Unable to stop the dog doing this, it had had to be put down.

Another male client arrived absolutely surrounded by spirit pigeons. He was an elderly man who had always been a pigeon fancier and gained great satisfaction from his hobby. The thought that his spirit birds still remembered him brought a lump to the throat.

Edith was able to pass a warning given to her by a spirit to a lady client. 'Tell your brother to do something about that dog Bindy,' she said. The lady was shocked. Her brother had indeed got a Staffordshire bull terrier named Bindy that had started having fits. Shortly afterwards the dog had to be put down.

One couple that visited Edith had recently had their dog put to sleep. It was old and frail and had to be carried outside to perform and back inside again. The poor animal had no life and distressing though it was for them, the kindest thing for its owners to do was let the vet administer that fatal dose. The dog came to Edith in spirit, putting thoughts and pictures into her head and she was able to tell its grieving owners that he liked the new wall unit they had just had fitted in the sitting room although to him it seemed gigantic. From a dog's perspective it would be, but the message brought great satisfaction to the broken-hearted owners.

Whatever you decide to do, I hope anyone who has lost a pet and is looking forward to being united again some day will take heart. Animals pass to the spirit world in exactly the same way that we do.

V

Dreams and Their Interpretations

They hide in your sleep,
as a slight weight on your chest
or in the sun as a four-footed shadow
in the corner of your eye
that when you turn to face
is only a bunch of flowers
bending in the wind

'Ghost Cats' by Scott T. Starbuck

Many pet-owners are thinking about their pet – physical or spiritual – when they fall asleep, and as the conscious brain looses control these thoughts are released. These are known as self-suggested dreams and just as our pets give us pleasure, so do the dreams. Close your eyes and hold the final image of your pet in your mind, so that it's the last thing you recall before sleeping. When you wake, close your eyes and allow the dream images to flow once more through your mind, then write them down quickly as they fade very fast after waking.

When we are on the verge of waking up, a hypnopompic state occurs and is characterised by dream-like images. Likewise, a hypnogogic image is experienced just before falling asleep and often takes the form of both visual and auditory hallucination. Many incidents that seem very real are logically acknowledged as being from these two states.

Moggy's Return

Kath Bower had been brought up with animals and had a particular liking for cats but unfortunately when she married John Morgan she had to abandon all ideas of having a cat of their own as John was allergic to cat-dander. The situation was made worse by the fact that only weeks after her wedding, Moggy, her childhood cat, died and she missed him terribly.

One night, she woke to hear an odd half-muffled 'mrrrr' and instinctively reached out in the darkness and felt a long-haired cat about the size and coat texture of Moggy. Her sharp intake of breath obviously aroused John who reached for the bedside light, and as the room was suddenly bathed in light, the feeling of the cat under her hand disappeared. Kath was understandably upset and the situation wasn't helped by John insisting it was a dream. Kath didn't argue. She remained adamant that Moggy actually returned that night and nothing John could say would change that.

Many owners dream about their deceased pets.

Childhood pets can return in spirit or in dreams.

Julia's Midnight Visitor

It was the middle of the night and Julia Connelly was waking up from a dream in which she was talking to an elderly man who was standing at the end of her bed. In her dream she woke up and saw the man, and then actually woke up and discovered that he was still standing there. A second later he melted slowly away. This had all the hallmarks of hypnopompic imagery – images seen during the potentially hallucinatory state between sleeping and waking, but it had given Julia a huge fright.

Unable to get back to sleep, she went to get Snuggles her pet cat, more for reassurance than protection against ghosts, but Snuggles wasn't normally allowed on the bed and instantly jumped off. She picked him up and carried him over to the bed again, but he wasn't happy and leapt off again. On the third attempt, he seemed to be settling. He padded round and round as cats do before settling down, then suddenly stopped and stood stock-still. He stared at the place where the man had been, then in one swift move, leapt off the bed and charged out of the room.

Was this just a coincidence? Julia tried to convince herself that she had been dreaming and Snuggles had seen a moth or insect that was invisible to her. It was possible, yet she couldn't dismiss the fact that the two incidents seemed to have some deeper, more mysterious link.

DREAM INTERPRETATIONS

When we sleep, our subconscious mind becomes active and we receive flashes of intuition and prophetic vision that lie hidden in depths which our conscious mind normally stifles.

Dreams may alert us to unconsidered possibilities and options, and this is not in any way weird or spooky. It is our unconscious mind giving us information that perhaps our conscious mind has not considered. Many dreams are spontaneous but you can structure them so that they will focus on a particular issue. The Ancient Greeks and Egyptians used a technique like our self-suggested dream, but they called it dream incubation. By focusing on a particular issue just before sleep, you are likely to obtain an answer while the mind is open to the more psychic sources of wisdom.

Many people believe that if we dream of animals, they represent our own characteristics, our primitive desires and sometimes our personality. They can also be symbolic. If an animal talks to you it suggests that you should unlock dormant potential. If you save an animal's life, you are being attributed with that animal's characteristics, but if you are fighting an animal, you are rejecting a part of yourself.

Dreams usually need an interpretation, so here is a key to unlocking your animal dreams.

DOMESTIC ANIMALS

Cat To see cats in your dreams can signify spiritual powers. To see a white cat means you are going through difficult times, but usually the colour or breed is insignificant. If in your dream, you see a cat walking alone, it signifies a journey. To see a meowing cat means lies will be told about you. If the cat is scratching itself you will be deceived. A purring cat means you will be guilty of hypocrisy.

But not all is doom and gloom. If you see your own beloved cat, it denotes an independent, creative spirit and feminine sexuality.

Dog To dream of your own dog is lucky; it denotes the fidelity of friends, a generous spirit, protection and intuition. It could also be a sign that you have forgotten a talent you once had and might need to re-activate.

To dream of strange dogs symbolises enemies who are waiting to ruin you. If you dream that a dog bites you on the leg, it indicates that you have lost the ability to balance certain aspects of your life. Yet surprisingly, mad dogs that attack and bite the dreamer are good omens foretelling the coming of influential and kindly strangers. If you dream that a dog speaks to you, you will learn something of great benefit to you from a friend.

To dream of following hounds is lucky, you will reap success. To dream of hunting wild animals is a good omen as it shows that you are fearless in life and will eventually meet with great success. However, if you are pursued by hounds, your marriage will be an unhappy one.

Horse, Ass and Donkey Dream of an ass and you will overcome your present affliction if you have the patience to wait a little longer. Slowly but surely, happiness is approaching. To ride a horse is a good dream foretelling the making of money and true friends. To fall off a horse denotes a hasty wedding. To beat one means your aims will be thwarted. To see a number of horses signifies independence and happiness, but beware of 'horsing around'.

BATS, BIRDS, BUTTERFLIES AND BEES

Bat If you dream of a bat flying at night, some unknown enemy may do you harm. If you dream that you see a bat by day, you will escape a danger that is threatening.

Bee To dream of a bee or bees is exceedingly fortunate as it foretells great domestic happiness, improvement in industry and faithfulness of friends. To dream that you are stung by a bee or a wasp tells of envious enemies who will attempt to dishonour you. If you see several wasps flying, a most unpleasant piece of news will shortly be communicated to you.

Birds On the wing predict an upward trend of affairs, bringing happiness and success.

Butterfly Not a favourable dream. It signifies that you are right in doubting the faithfulness of your lover.

Cuckoo A sign of troubles in love which will result in quarrels and the arrival of a new lover. If the bird is heard and not seen, you will be deceived by someone who pretends to give you good advice.

Dove Experience peace and tranquillity, but if the dove drops to the ground, it foretells the death of a distant relative. To dream of a pigeon flying is a propitious sign indicating good news from abroad and a happy surprise at home. If they are roosting, your marriage partner will be faithful and you will live in peace and harmony.

Eagle Flying high means your ambitions will be realised. If the eagle is nesting or coming down to earth, you will meet with disappointment both in business and love.

Lark Denotes great joy and exhilaration, a happy partner in marriage, and an abundance of all the good things in life.

Magpie The omen of a hasty and unhappy marriage.

Partridge A covey of partridges is a sign of misfortune, but a single bird in the air is exceedingly lucky and foretells prosperity. A sitting partridge predicts that you will have an angry rebuke from a friend.

Peacock An unfortunate dream indicating loss of money and many heartaches.

Seagulls On the wing, news from abroad will follow shortly, but if the seagulls are on the water, the news will be bad.

Sparrows If you are feeding them, great domestic happiness will be yours. If, however, the birds fly away from you, you will receive an unpleasant surprise concerning household matters.

Starlings You will be rebuked by a friend because of an unjust action on your part.

Swan If it is white, it foretells great happiness in marriage and several children. A black swan denotes a handsome marriage partner.

FARMYARD ANIMALS

Bull If the bull is charging you, enemies are slandering you. If the bull is eating peacefully in the field, there is great prosperity in store for the dreamer.

Cock and *Hen* If the cock crows in your dream, a false friend is planning to do you harm. A silent cock indicates a rival in love who is more formidable than you expect. To dream of a cackling hen signifies future joy, but a silent one spells sorrow. To pluck a hen means financial gain; to see one with its chicks means loss and damage.

Goose Your expectations will end in disappointment. If you kill the goose, you will achieve startling success.

Lamb A lucky dream signifying peace and health. More than one lamb, an addition to the family. Should you dream of a shepherd, that is a good omen as it presages business successes and the disappearance of worries.

Sheep To see a flock of sheep feeding in a dream denotes a faithful lover, but if you see sheep enclosed in a pen it signifies a disappointment.

Turkey You will be involved in trouble due to some mistake which you have made, but the consequences of it will have a beneficial effect on your life.

WILD ANIMALS

If you dream you are visiting a zoo, it foretells a change of employment which will bring you much profit and pleasure. To dream of wild animals, especially the big cats, signifies cruelty and treachery on the part of your enemies.

Ape An ape in your dream will signify ill-fortune as a result of malicious slander.

Bear If you are running from the bear, your present happiness is shortly to be marred by a rich, unscrupulous enemy. If you slay the bear, you will prevail against your enemy.

Deer If deer run from you as you approach, you will deeply offend your friends by some action. If the deer come towards you, there will be a reconciliation with a former lover.

Fox Dream of a fox and you need to take action quickly. It signifies that you have a competitor or rival who can only be outwitted if you take immediate action.

Leopard A rather unlucky dream. You will have to fight against many malicious influences before success comes your way.

Lion The king of the jungle symbolises great strength of character, power and aggression. You will rise in power, but when you do, use this power carefully, especially in relation to your friends who have been instrumental in helping you.

Mouse This foretells busybodies who will attempt to interfere with your affairs. Don't allow them to do so; act as you see fit. To dream of a rat signifies secret and powerful enemies, but if you kill the rat, you will defeat them.

Owl A melancholy dream predicting sadness, poverty and sometimes disgrace.

Spider If you dream about a spider it means you will have a lucky escape from an accident, but if you see a spider spinning, you will receive a sum of money.

Tiger A warning dream, presaging the arrival of one who will attempt to harm you.

Wolf The sign of a treacherous friend who will tell many lies in order to bring discredit to you.

Zebra A change in circumstances; poverty followed by a successful business transaction which will bring riches.

SNAKES AND SLIMIES

Adder To dream of being bitten by an adder means that lies and treachery will be coming from a false friend. To kill one indicates the end of an undesirable friendship.

Alligator Dream of an alligator and someone in your circle of acquaintances is a sly and treacherous enemy. You will recognise the person from the exaggerated friendship he displays in an attempt to win your favour and confidence.

Ants If they are hard at work on the ant-hill, it is auspicious for those that are engaged in industry, foretelling increased prosperity and expansion of business. Lovers may expect a happy wedded life following this dream. If the ants are flying, the dreamer will journey to a foreign land or pay a visit to a large town.

   If you stamp on or in some way destroy an ant it is an ill omen, indicating that your carefully laid plans will result in utter failure and destruction.

Fish If you are successful and catch many fish, you have ambitions that will soon be realised. No catch at all indicates loss or failure. To see a single fish is a lucky dream as it denotes increased prosperity, a devoted spouse and a brilliant child. If several fish are swimming, many friends are working to help you.

Frog To dream of a frog is lucky. It denotes profit for the trader, good crops for the farmer, victories for the soldier and sailor, and a happy marriage for the lover.

Lizard An unfortunate dream implying bad luck lasting the next few days. A dishonest business friend may cause you trouble for a time.

Snail Both a good and a bad dream. It foreshadows a letter bearing good news, but also a conversation which could result in tears.

Snakes Do you have hidden fears and worries? Maybe you have enemies? Face up to them, because with strength and courage you can prevail against them.

Toad This is giving you warning of something you must avoid, so if you are tempted to go off the rails or be dishonest – don't.

Turtles A sign that you are moving too fast and not paying attention to detail, so slow down, relax and come out of that shell of yours.

Weasel Beware. You will meet an extremely snide person and the situation could spell danger, so take care.

Worms Be prepared. Numerous small, niggly worries are awaiting you but don't let them get out of context. Look at the big picture and you'll realise they are tiny and of no consequence in the overall state of things.

VI

PROTECTIVE DOGS AND PHANTOM PROTECTORS

Many people decide to have a dog for protection, but some dogs have an amazing loyalty to their owners and take their duties extremely seriously. Dogs have always been used to guard property and people, but why would a dog risk his own life to save his master, or stay with an injured master? What made Ruswarp and Tip choose to stay to guard the bodies of their dead masters for months until they were eventually found collapsed and starving? Is it a desire to continue to serve and protect that draws animals to the graves of those they love? Even after death, dogs are there for our protection.

Rigel's Titanic Rescue
Rigel, a huge black Newfoundland dog owned by First Officer Murdoch, was with his master on the fateful night when the *Titanic* sank and became a pet hero by saving the lives of passengers and crew in Lifeboat Four.

During the night the lifeboat was drifting aimlessly into the path of the rescue steamer, the SS *Carpathia*, and was in danger of being crushed when Rigel raised the alarm. He had been swimming in the icy water in front of the lifeboat for three hours, yet he began to bark, alerting the crew of the *Carpathia* to the plight of the tiny vessel.

The passengers and Rigel were transferred to the rescue steamer, but Rigel refused to leave the lifeboat deck. He stayed at the ship's rail staring mournfully out to sea, looking for his drowned master.

The Faithful Ruswarp
The bond between dog and owner is often so strong that many dogs will stand guard over their dead masters.

On 20 January 1990, Graham Nuttall went walking in the Elan Valley in Wales accompanied by his fourteen-year-old cross collie Ruswarp. When he didn't return, the police were alerted, but despite a search, the pair were never found. Three months later, on 7 April, a rambler found Ruswarp collapsed and starving on a remote hillside, lying by the body of his dead master.

The Devotion of Tip
On 12 December 1953, Tip and her master Joseph Tagg, an eighty-one-year-old gamekeeper from Bamford, Derbyshire set out to walk along Howden moors but, in the middle of nowhere, Mr Tagg collapsed and died. When the two did not return, search parties were sent out but

Is this phantom dog protecting the child in the pedal car as this 1950 photograph would indicate?

failed to find them and the harsh weather conditions hampered all their attempts. Through the bleak winter months of severe frost and snow storms, everyone presumed them to be dead, yet unknown to them faithful Tip stayed by her dead master's body until a couple of men rounding up stray sheep found them fifteen weeks later.

Carried down from the moors, Tip's survival was nothing short of miraculous and although her emaciated body was in poor health she lived another year with a niece of Joseph Tagg. She was awarded a bronze medal, the highest order of canine chivalry, and she was even featured in a traditional Derbyshire well-dressing scene, but her ordeal had been too great. She died a year later of 16 February 1955 and was buried on the moors where she had kept her faithful vigil. Her loyalty touched the heart of people everywhere and a year after her death a memorial shrine was unveiled on the roadside close by the dam wall of Derwent reservoir.

When a person dies, we can sometimes forget how deeply a bereaved animal may be suffering because of the loss. Given kindness, understanding and care, the animal may settle in time, but some animals may not survive the loss of an owner.

Mac's Last Moments

When Harold King died, he left behind a Scottie named Mac. A family friend took Mac to live with him, but the dog became restless and ill. They took him to a vet but next morning Mac disappeared. Two days later the caretaker of the cemetery where Harold King was buried found Mac's body on top of his master's grave. What strange instinct told Mac he was going to die and how did he find his master's grave? The only way seems to be through a deep, telepathic bond.

What magnet of the heart drew Flin to his master's grave?

Flin Finds His Master's Grave

When Martin Dell died, his old dog Flin would not be comforted. He barely ate and wandered round the house and garden sniffing and whining. The Dell family found the dog's distress hard to bear in addition to their own, yet nothing would comfort him. Then one day, despite showing no previous interest in going out of the garden, he simply disappeared and for days there was no sign of him.

A week later, the family went to place flowers on Martin's grave. It was a remote cemetery about three miles from their home in a district they had only previously passed through, yet there, pacing back and forth like a sentry, was Flin.

Despite the fact that he was delighted to see his old family, when they tried to leave with him, Flin refused to be pulled, picked up, carried or placed in the car. Eventually they arranged for the caretaker to feed and care for him and left him with his old master.

Greyfriar's Bobby

The story of Greyfriar's Bobby is perhaps the most widely know story of loyalty shown by a dog. Bobby was a black Skye terrier who, with his shepherd Auld Jock, herded sheep on Cauldbrae Farm in the Pentland Hills in southern Scotland. Every Wednesday Jock, with Bobby at his heels, went into Edinburgh to the market, and punctually at 1.00 p.m. they would have lunch at Traill's Dining Rooms in Greyfriar's Place.

Then one day in 1858, Jock was sacked from his job and driven away from the farm, but Bobby would not stay without Jock and set off to find him. Locating him in a dirty alley in Edinburgh, the two of them spent the night together, but next morning Jock was dead. He was buried in Greyfriar's churchyard. Three days later at exactly 1.00 p.m., a hungry Bobby appeared at Traill's Dining Rooms. John Traill recognised the little dog and gave him a bone. When Bobby appeared again the following day, John Traill decided to follow him when he left, and Bobby led him straight to Greyfriar's churchyard and the grave of Auld Jock.

John Traill made arrangements for Bobby to be returned to Cauldbrae Farm, but within days, Bobby had returned to the grave.

Several people, including John Traill, tried to adopt him but Bobby howled pitifully until he was allowed to return to Greyfriar's churchyard. For the next nine years, Bobby kept up his lonely vigil, only leaving the grave at 1.00 p.m. each day to go to Traill's Dining Rooms for food.

Then in their wisdom the local authorities decided the law was being broken and Bobby was taken to court for being unlicensed (every dog needed a 7s 6d licence until the 1970s). Bobby was declared a vagrant and John Traill was imprisoned for harbouring him, but the case caused so

The statue of Greyfriar's Bobby, the faithful Skye terrier.

much publicity that the Lord Provost of Edinburgh, William Chambers, adopted Bobby, paid his licence fee and gave him the freedom of the city. He was also given a new collar on which was inscribed 'Greyfriars Bobby, from the Lord Provost – licensed'!

Bobby died in January 1872 and John Traill had him buried in a flowerbed near Greyfriar's churchyard. A memorial statue of Greyfriar's Bobby was commissioned by Baroness Burdett Coutts and still stand above a drinking fountain on the corner of Candlemaker Row and George VI Bridge. His collar is in the Huntley House Museum in Canongate. The grave of his master is now marked by a headstone, but although Traill's Dining Rooms no longer exist, it is commemorated at 6 Greyfriar's Place with a brass plate on the door which reads 'Greyfriar's Bobby was fed here 1858–1872'.

PHANTOM PROTECTORS OR GUARDIAN ANGELS
The phantom protectors in this section show that the spirits of certain animals survive the death process and are still there for our protection.

The Mystery Minder
A young woman was travelling on foot in a remote country area of the Peak District late one dark night. There were no street lights or pavements, and the hedges and overhanging trees formed strange shapes and made even stranger noises as she hurried past. Her imagination was playing tricks and she was quaking with fear as she almost ran headlong into a large dog that seemed to appear from nowhere. Although usually afraid of dogs, she found this one friendly and comforting, and it stayed by her side until the lights of houses were reached when, with a wag of its tail, it went its own way, disconcertingly disappearing through a solid stone wall.

The Minister's Mate
A Methodist minister was walking along the road from Calver Sough to Stoney Middleton one night when he realised he was being followed. He was carrying the collection money from the various chapels he served and felt rather vulnerable until he was unexpectedly joined by a large dog that stayed protectively by his heels until he reached his destination. Reaching down to stroke the dog, his hand passed straight through it.

Phantom protectors continue to be there when needed.

Kath's Escort

Living in a city suburb, Kath's regular route home meant walking through an underpass. Often she would walk the long way round in order to avoid using the underpass, particularly at night, because the dimly lit tunnel made her feel rather uneasy. On one dark night, she felt too exhausted to take the long route, so pushing her anxiety to the back of her mind she marched determinedly down the steps and entered the tunnel. Almost immediately she spotted the silhouette of a medium-sized dog that frisked up to her then started to walk through the tunnel alongside her.

Somehow this unexpected escort gave her courage and when they reached the end of the tunnel she said a few words to the dog, who wagged his tail. She reached down to pat him but as she did so her hand made no contact as it met only empty air. She blinked in disbelief but the dog had vanished.

The Phantom Escorts

These are not unusual occurrences. A woman from north Staffordshire told of how late one evening she had been escorted part of the way home by a large black dog. Although she admitted that she hadn't actually seen the dog, she was aware of its presence as she had felt it sniff her hand. It could be passed off as an overactive mind, yet the fact that she was not an imaginative woman gave the situation added credulity.

A lady from Two Dales, Derbyshire, who didn't believe in ghosts, was escorted by a large black dog who padded quietly beside her as she walked down Sydnope Hill one dark night. 'What are you doing out here?' she asked the dog. 'Get off home.' The dog promptly disappeared.

The Ghost Sheepdog

This is a story from the December 1964 edition of the *Derbyshire Life and Countryside*, but sadly there are no details of where the encounter took place or the names of the people involved.

One winter's evening, a man went into a public house in a lonely part of the hills of the High Peak. The bar was deserted apart from a large black and white collie dog lounging by the welcoming fire. After the man had called to the dog without response, a farmer entered the bar and the landlord emerged to serve his two customers. Shortly afterwards, with drink in hand, the customer turned back to the fire, but the dog had disappeared.

'That's funny,' said the man turning to the others. 'I was just going to ask if the dog was friendly, but he seems to have gone.'

The farmer and the landlord looked at each other, then asked 'What dog?'

The visitor described the dog, whereupon the farmer hurriedly downed his drink and left.

'He's gone to fetch the sheep down to lower pastures,' the landlord told the visitor. 'That ghost dog always appears when there is going to be a bad snowfall.'

Apparently many years previously, the dog and his owner froze to death in a fierce blizzard while trying to round up their mountain flock. Since the tragedy, each time a heavy snowfall is due, the ghost of the dog appears as a warning to others who might meet the same fate.

Gerigio, the Phantom Dog of Turin

This is the famous story of Gerigio, the phantom dog of Turin who loyally protected a priest named Don Bosco who had dedicated his life to improving the lot of the urchins of Turin in the mid-nineteenth century.

Don Bosco lived in a hostel in the Valdacco quarter, the most dangerous slum district of Turin. It attracted all the dregs of the city and the town's ruffians, and was a dangerous place to be.

In carrying out his work, Don Bosco made many enemies. Some were even prepared to kill him to prevent him continuing his good deeds, but whenever he was in trouble, the huge, grey, wolf-like frame of an unknown dog appeared out of nowhere to save his life or help him through a crisis. The dog, named Gerigio, would then escort Don Bosco back to the Pinardi house where he lived, but as the door closed, he would trot off into the darkness and disappear.

Frequently Gerigio would be waiting outside the door as Don Bosco was about to set out on an evening errand, or was about to return home alone, but one evening as Don Bosco left the hostel, he found Gerigio stretched out in front of the door, blocking his way.

Don Bosco gave the dog a friendly pat and tried to move him, but Gerigio refused to move and growled ominously as the priest tried to push past. Don Bosco was both surprised and dismayed at this change in Gerigio and finally gave up the idea of trying to force his way past the snarling dog. Moments later, a breathless friend ran up, and as Gerigio ambled away, Don Bosco was told of an attempt on his life that had been planned for that night. Gerigio's delaying action had saved the priest's life again.

The first of these incidents occurred in the autumn of 1852 and the last in 1883, covering a period of over thirty years, twice the life expectancy of a normal dog. During this time, there were many stray dogs roaming the city of Turin, hungry and abandoned, yet Gerigio never ate or drank and no-one discovered where he came from or where he went to.

Over the years, many people have tried to explain the mysteries of this phantom dog; one of the most likely explanations being that Gerigio was Don Bosco's guardian angel who took on the appearance of a dog when necessary.

The Phantom Guard Dog

A guardian angel in canine form chose to help Lucy Crich of Lincoln. While her husband worked on the nightshift she was never afraid of being at home at night with her two small children, in fact she very rarely even bothered to lock the doors, despite neighbours warning her to do so.

One evening she had just brought the washing in from off the clothes line and as she pushed the door closed, the Yale lock clicked into place. Although surprised by this, she took this as a reminder to lock the front door too. It was then that she heard a throaty growling outside, and peering through the window she saw a strange dog sitting by her doorstep. As she watched, the dog's hackles rose and looking in the direction it was staring, she saw a man lurking in the

Could this be a guardian angel in canine form?

shadows. She instinctively knew he was up to no good, but rooted to the spot in terror she watched as he inched towards the house.

Then just as he neared the door, the dog pounced, the man let out a scream and man and dog fell to the ground. The man wrenched himself free and ran, but the dog calmly walked away and disappeared.

Everyone raised sceptical eyebrows when Lucy told them what had happened, but she remained firmly convinced that the dog had been her guardian angel sent to protect her and her young family.

VII

GHOST ANIMALS

The Cottage Cat

Having moved into a period cottage in Cromford, the new occupants decided to have a stylish bathroom installed, and as they were both out at work all day, they gave the builders a key for convenience. As well as being concerned about the installation and the mess, they also asked the builders if they would try to keep the noise down so that their elderly neighbour was not disturbed.

When the job was finished and the builders returned the key, they told the couple they had been so quiet they hadn't even disturbed the cat sleeping on the bed.

'But we don't have a cat,' said the couple, thinking that a neighbour's cat must have sneaked in. 'What did it look like?'

'It was all grey,' replied the builder.

The couple had never seen a grey cat and despite making numerous enquiries, found that no-one owned or had seen a grey cat in the area. Then the elderly neighbour remembered that the old lady who had lived in the house had had a grey cat for many years. Was this that same cat that was grounded in its old home?

The Cat's Return

Sometimes animal ghosts are only visible to other animals as this story shows.

When she was a child, Angela Read remembers her father uncovering the skeleton of a cat while digging in their garden. It had no doubt been the pet of a former owner of the house so the animal was re-interred. Shortly afterwards, the family began hearing a cat's footsteps padding around the house. Although cats are very light footed, these footsteps seemed to be strangely amplified. Then, their cat Twink started acting strangely. His fur would hackle and he'd spit and stare at a corner of the room as if some alien cat had invaded his territory.

A while later, after Twink's death, the family acquired a lively, playful kitten called Tom who gradually grew into a lively, playful cat. He was extremely self-absorbed and seemed to chase, roll and play as if with an invisible friend. His play-fights brimmed with enthusiasm and were accompanied by an increasing amount of vocalization as he constantly seemed to swap roles from attacker to defender.

'Perhaps he's playing with that ghost cat,' suggested a friend as they watched him play. It was a comforting thought that Tom had a playmate but rather unnerving that no-one but Tom could see it.

Above left: Nothing disturbed the ghost cat sleeping on the bed.

Above right: Spirit cats and dogs often hang around their old homes where they were loved.

This photograph was taken during the First World War by Arthur Springer, a retired Scotland Yard detective. The ladies were taking tea in the garden of a house in Tingewick, Buckinghamshire, yet there was no dog present.

The Persistent Puss

Jose and her husband Douglas were away for the weekend staying at an idyllic country house hotel, an old moted manor house in the heart of Bury St Edmunds. On the first evening they were getting ready for bed when they heard distinct scratching at the door of their room. It was no doubt the cat or dog of the house that was most likely allowed into the room when it was not occupied. It probably slept on the bed, but neither Jose nor Douglas had any desire to share their bed with a strange animal, so after commenting about the marks being made on the paintwork, they tried to ignore the scratching.

But the animal was insistent and eventually, having had enough, Douglas marched over to the door intending to shoo it away. He threw open the door but there was no animal there and the corridor was deserted. The animal had obviously heard his approaching footsteps and in anticipation of being reprimanded had run away quickly – perhaps a little too quickly.

They were not disturbed again that evening, but next day they mentioned the incident to the owners of the hotel who assured them they did not have a dog or a cat and had never had one during the whole time they had lived there. Feeling rather perplexed, Jose asked if it was possible that another guest had brought their dog? No, they were assured; dogs were not allowed in the hotel.

Unconvinced, they checked the door for scratches and telltale grooves in the paintwork. There were none. If Jose had been the only one to hear the scratching, she might have had doubts, but how could they account for the fact that they had both clearly heard it, there were no marks on the door and the animal had vanished very quickly.

The Ghost Monkey of Athelhampton Hall

It may be a co-incidence that the crest of the Martyn family of Athelhampton Hall in Dorset was an ape sitting on a tree stump, because it is said that the ghost of a monkey haunts the hall now.

Apparently a daughter of the family was jilted in love and in her distraught state climbed a stairway behind a secret doorway in the Great Chamber to a room where she committed suicide. Sadly the family's pet monkey had followed her, and as neither the body of the girl nor the monkey were found in time, the trapped little creature starved to death. Now people hear the ghostly sound of it scratching the panelling of the secret stairway in a desperate attempt to escape.

The Snoring Dog

Janice Rice went to stay overnight with her friend in Durham, but during the night was woken by the sound of snoring. Thinking it was her hostess, who was asleep in the room next door, she turned over and eventually went back to sleep. Next morning, Janice made a joke of her friend's snoring, but was told it was not her, but her dog who had always slept in her bedroom. The dog had been dead several years but his astral presence and his habit of snoring seemed to have remained.

The Whining Dog

The weather had turned bad and snow was falling thickly at a remote farmhouse in the Peak District. The farmer knew the area well, but his visitor was a stranger. To let him try to make the journey back to Buxton on such a night would have been madness, so the visitor was offered a bed for the night on the couch in the living room.

He settled down quite comfortably, grateful for the offer, and before long he was fast asleep. But his rest was short-lived and he couldn't get back to sleep for the continual whining of a dog

Above: A snoring ghost?

Right: Did the presence of a little girl in the room bring back a childhood pet?

that seemed to be in the room with him. Eventually he could stand it no longer and decided to put the animal in the neighbouring kitchen, yet despite a search he could find no dog. Thinking the animal was playing tricks with him, the visitor made several attempts to catch the dog, but without success.

Next morning, the exhausted visitor told the farmer, who shook his head in confusion. They had had no dog since their old sheepdog had died two years earlier, but eventually came to the conclusion that the presence of a stranger in the house could have brought him back in spirit to guard his old home.

The Dog's Return

When she was a child, Emma remembers going with her family to visit an aunt and uncle in Hertfordshire. They stayed overnight and Emma was given her cousin Sarah's room, as being much older Sarah was away at college. The room was still full of her cuddly toys and childhood favourites and Emma was allowed to play with the toys before going to sleep.

But during the night, Emma kept being disturbed because a soft-coated dog kept jumping onto her bed. Emma was not sure this was such a good idea and kept pushing the dog off, but it took at least five rejections before the dog finally gave up.

Next morning Emma asked where the dog was, but her aunt stared at her in amazement as she told her they didn't have a dog. When Emma described what had happened they all looked at each other in disbelief. The dog Emma described was a shih-tzu who had been Sarah's constant companion throughout her childhood and had died shortly before she left home. Had the presence of a little girl in the room brought the spirit of Sarah's childhood pet back?

The Invisible Friend

A child's imaginary friend is more often than not a companion of similar age, yet here is another exception. Gillian's invisible friend was a dog called Trixie. For many years, this doggy spirit was allowed to sleep on Gillian's bed, sit with her while watching television, be fed at the table, and accompany her everywhere. It was not until around the time of Gillian's ninth birthday that talk of Trixie grew less and less, then eventually she disappeared entirely.

The Holiday Experience

Jean and Richard Low were on holiday in Southern Ireland in 1994. They were staying in Clifton, County Galway, a quiet west-coast town where nothing much happens. It was lunchtime and as Jean and Richard strolled down the high street, looking for a place to eat, the town was deserted apart from a few farmers seeking a liquid lunch. They paused at an old pub. The menu looked good so they stepped inside and found themselves in a smoky bar off which was the rather gloomy restaurant.

They seated themselves at a small table with Jean facing the door to the bar and as they waited, a large black Labrador ambled over and sat down beside Jean. She reached down to touch it but her hand moved through the air without making any contact with the animal.

Jean is a Christian spiritualist, a clairvoyant and clairsensient who believes in the spirit world, so this rather unnerving experience did not unduly bother her as she calmly told Richard what had just happened. Richard was disappointed that he had been unable to see the dog and they were discussing this when a waitress arrived at their table. Jean related what had occurred and the waitress nodded knowingly. Apparently the dog appeared regularly, made contact, then simply faded away.

The Visitor Who Saw the Ghostly Cat

As a nine year old, Ben remembers going to a friend's large old house on the Isle of White. They were playing in the boy's bedroom when through the open door to the landing Ben noticed what he thought was a black cat, and mentioned this to his friend.

'We don't have a cat,' said his friend sounding rather agitated.

'But I saw it,' Ben persisted and walked out of the room to check. Sure enough there it was at the top of the stairs, but as his friend approached the animal dashed downstairs. Ben called down to the friend's mother who was in the sitting room, to ask if she had seen the strange cat. She seemed very upset and angry and told the boys to go back into the bedroom immediately and stop playing around the stairs.

Half an hour later Ben's parents arrived to take him home although it had been arranged for him to stay over. Ben figured he must have upset his friend's mother somehow and this was her way of punishing the boys for playing round the stairs.

It was many years later that Ben discovered that the house had been haunted by black creatures of varying sizes that had not only terrorised the family, but attacked them too. What Ben had seen was one of those creatures and a phone call from his friend's distressed mother had brought his parents into a panic. It did however bring matters to a head as the house was exorcised and the family had no further problems.

The Dog on the Footpath

Just occasionally, a human is able to see a ghost animal that another animal is completely oblivious to. That's what happened to Leonard Short as he walked his dog Roy. On the footpath ahead of them he noticed a black dog standing in the middle of the path. He was thankful he'd seen it before Roy, who was a rather antisocial dog, and Leonard was able to clip Roy's lead on before he reacted to the stranger. As they walked closer, Leonard waited for the expected pull when Roy spotted the other dog, but surprisingly he didn't pull, bark or show any signs of aggression. In fact, Roy was ignoring the dog completely, which was very unusual for him. He walked past as if it wasn't even there, so Leonard removed the lead and Roy shot off, escorted by the other dog. Leonard watched them run together for at least thirty seconds before he lost sight of them, then Roy came charging back alone. The other dog was nowhere in sight and the strange thing was, Roy hadn't acted aggressively or made a sound during the whole encounter. It was as if the other dog just hadn't existed.

Haunted Veterinary Practices

Because people die in hospitals, they are places often associated with ghosts, and the same can be said for animal hospitals and veterinary practices.

Jacqui lived in a flat above a veterinary practice in Rotherham and always had a strange feeling that the place was haunted by spirit presences. Her predecessor had obviously felt the same because when Jacqui moved in she found a makeshift altar with holy water, a bible and some candles. Considering this to be stuff and nonsense, Jacqui tipped the water away, gave the bible to a charity shop and burnt the candles.

A lab technician working in one animal hospital reported seeing disappearing ghost cats in the waiting room, hearing paws and nails hitting the floor and even seeing a floating light that moved across the room before disappearing.

Nigger, the Dambusters' Loyal Mascot

During the Second World War, there were many airfields in Lincolnshire. The 617 Dambuster Squadron were based at Scampton and at the nearby Petwood Hotel, which used to be the officers' mess, the ghost of Wing Commander Guy Gibson VC has been seen accompanied by his faithful black Labrador Nigger.

Nigger (a popular name for a black dog, but not now PC) was adopted by 617 as its mascot until Nigger was killed by a car on 16 May 1943. He was buried at RAF Scampton and it seems that he still haunts the airfield. A black Labrador has been frequently seen running soundlessly about the airfield's perimeter fencing, but disappears when approached.

When the Dambusters' Memorial was officially opened in nearby Woodhall Spa in May 1987, the choir from St Hilda's School sang before posing for a photograph in front of the memorial. Suddenly, a black Labrador appeared and sat down in the middle of the group. He belonged to no-one present, yet refused to leave until the photographs had been taken, then he simply disappeared, leaving people to ask, 'Was that Nigger, the Dambusters' loyal mascot?'

Borley Rectory's Canine Ghosts

Borley Rectory near Sudbury on the Suffolk/Essex border had the reputation of being the most haunted house in England, although it might be more fair to say that it was the most investigated and written about haunted house in England. Along with all the other ghostly activities here, noises were reported that sounded like the pattering of a large dog walking along a corridor and what seemed to be the panting of an invisible dog.

The White Ghost Dog

At Stocken Hall Farm in Rutlandshire, the ghost of a little white dog has been seen many times. Often people open doors for it, only to find that it has suddenly disappeared. Once, the then occupant of the house and her daughter were going up a narrow staircase when the dog passed them. They both felt it stroke them as it passed between them and the jamb of the door at the top of the stairs, but this time it was invisible. For hours afterwards they both experienced a burning chill where it had touched them.

Borley Rectory had such a plethora of ghosts, including panting dogs.

The Fowl Ghost

Perhaps the most bizarre animal ghost story is that associated with Pendragon Castle in Cumbria where a rich treasure is supposed to be buried in the castle's foundations. According to legend, any attempt to dig up the treasure will be thwarted by a huge spectral black hen that will scratch and peck at the pile of earth until any excavation work is filled in again.

The Spectral Blackbird

West Drayton church in Middlesex had a remarkable haunting that lasted one hundred years. People heard a peculiar knocking sound which seemed to emulate from the vaults under the church and when they peered through the grating they could see a great blackbird perched on one of the coffins inside, pecking away furiously. The parish clerk, his wife and daughter had all seen the bird, which usually appeared on a Friday evening.

One Friday evening when bell-ringers arrived at the church for a practise, they were met by a boy who was agitated by a blackbird he had seen flying round the chancel. Four of the bell-ringers and two of the youths armed with sticks and stones went to search for the mysterious bird. They found it fluttering amongst the rafters. One missile hit the bird, causing one of its wings to droop as if crippled, then finally, under a fusillade of blows, it fell wounded, fluttering into the eastern end of the church.

Two of the assailants immediately drove it into a corner and vaulted over the communion rail to seize it as it sank to the floor, but as the men thrust out their hands to seize it, the bird

A howling she-wolf of France haunts Castle Rising in Norfolk.

vanished. Local people believe the spectral bird is the restless and miserable spirit of a murderer who committed suicide and was buried at the north side of the churchyard.

The She-Wolf of France

On wild, wet nights, unearthly screams and howls have been heard from Castle Rising in Norfolk. They are said to come from the tormented soul of Queen Isabella, nicknamed the 'She-wolf of France'. Blamed for plotting the death of her husband, Edward II, her son avenged his father's death by keeping his mother imprisoned at Castle Rising where eventually she went mad.

Apparently her insane cries still reverberate around the castle. Some people claim she actually lives up to her name by returning in the form of a huge wolf with red eyes, blood dripping from its fangs and a howl to wake the dead.

Who Moved the Horses?

Many inexplicable incidents have happened at Furnace Mill, Lamberhurst, Kent, but from our point of view the strangest animal tale happened in May 1906 when Mr J.C. Playfair discovered that all his horses in the stables had been turned round. Their tails were in their mangers and their heads were where their tails should have been. One horse was missing altogether, and was found in a hayloft, but the doorway was too small to allow it to leave. In fact it was barely wide enough for a man to enter, so a partition had to be knocked down to get the horse out. How it had got there remains a complete mystery.

Who Put the Dog in the Cat's Cage

At a seventeenth-century home in Devon featured in *Most Haunted*, the Living TV programme, a family's pet cat usually slept in a cage in the kitchen and the dog roamed free. One morning when the family entered the kitchen, they found the dog in the cage and the cat roaming free. The cage door was fastened securely and a chair had been placed in front of the door.

Dogs in Historic Properties

Conisbrough Castle in Yorkshire was built primarily as a fortress but its unusual 27m (90ft) keep is circular, and was the inspiration for Sir Walter Scott's *Ivanhoe*.

In these early medieval buildings, it was customary as a ritual sacrifice to secrete a dog or cat within the walls, which at Conisbrough Castle are 4.6m (15ft) thick at the base. This was done predominantly in the area of the chapel, in the belief that the animal would ward off evil, a fact that is not usually known to visitors who regularly report hearing a dog howling mournfully around the chapel area.

Similar phenomena takes place at many other historic properties. At Bolsover Castle in Derbyshire, the skeleton of a dog believed to be over 500 years old was uncovered during recent renovation work and the spirit dog is now said to howl plaintively at night.

The ghostly sound of animals is often heard, as the above stories show, yet it is unusual to actually see one of these little creatures. However, there have been numerous sightings of a ginger tomcat at Lanercost Priory, set in the once turbulent borderland between England and Scotland. Apparently the cat, sometimes seen as a soft, orange light, walks through the transept and likes to rest on a tabletop tomb, but if approached will vanish into thin air.

The superstitious medieval builders who secreted a cat or dog in the walls of their buildings were also responsible for the dog-tooth pattern often found carved in the stone of ecclesiastical archways. This had the same symbolic purpose, to ward off evil, but was less barbaric, and no doubt just as effective. It was used extensively in the Early English style of architecture of twelfth/thirteenth-century Gothic.

The Ghostly Canine Companion

Many stately homes have their animal ghosts, the most common being the canine companions that escort the ghostly lady of the house.

The trim ghostly figure of a lady in white haunts Elvaston Castle in Derby. She is believed to be Maria Foote, a Covent Garden actress who married 'Beau' Pettersham, later the 4th Earl of Harrington, but was kept a recluse at their stately home. Now, this pitiful wraith is frequently seen accompanied by a large, white, spectral dog in the grounds of the castle.

King Charles's Ghostly Spaniels

Carisbrooke Castle on the Isle of Wight is a twelfth-century fortress where Charles I was held prisoner in 1647 before being taken to London for his trial and execution. As he walked down Whitehall to his execution, his little spaniel Rogue walked along beside him. After the execution, one of the Roundheads took the dog and exhibited him in the city.

King Charles's room at Carisbrooke Castle is now a popular tourist attraction, furnished as it would have been at the time. Whilst there, he was comfortably accommodated. A bowling green was constructed for his recreation, and he would have been allowed to have his dogs with him too. King Charles had a great fondness for those graceful little Spaniels that are named after him, so I was delighted to find that dogs are amongst the ghosts that have been seen at Carisbrooke Castle.

A lady in period dress is said to glide around the castle with two shadowy dogs on leashes, and in the courtyard another lady has been seen with four lapdogs. Could these be Cavalier King Charles spaniels, named after their patron, King Charles I? These apparitions could even be his beloved pets that kept him company in his last weeks at Carisbrooke Castle.

Charles II had the same love for the breed and took several dogs with him wherever he went. In fact he gave them the freedom of every public building in the land. Recently a breeder decided to put this to the test when she tried to gain entry to the Houses of Parliament but was refused admittance by the policeman on the door. She was unable to prove that this law ever existed but created a lot of publicity.

Cavalier King Charles spaniels and other similar small dogs appear in tapestries and in early portraits of the aristocratic families of Europe. Queen Elizabeth and many ladies of her court had small dogs to keep them warm in their large, draughty houses. It was not fashionable to wash or bath, so personal hygiene left a lot to be desired and fleas were all too common. The nobility hoped that the dog would become host to the fleas, which may account for the dog acquiring the name 'comforter' around this time.

'The Lost Beauty', an 1837 pencil drawing by James Bateman of a Cavalier King Charles spaniel.

Above: The ghost of Rudolph Valentino's dog has allegedly been seen in a Los Angeles cemetery.

Left: Henrietta d'Orleans, in this painting after P. Mignard, is seen with her Blenheim-coloured spaniel in around 1665. These little dogs, known as 'comforters', were very popular among noble ladies.

Last Wishes

To have the companionship of her pets in another world was obviously the intention behind the last wish of author Ellen Glasgow. She stipulated that on her death, her two pet dogs should be exhumed from her backyard and buried with her in a Hollywood cemetery. This was done, and many now claim that they have heard these dogs scampering round the grave late at night, and drivers have reported picking up the black forms of dogs in their headlights.

There are also reports of ghostly animals playing at Los Angeles pet cemetery. This houses the dead pets of many movie stars and famous people, and numerous people have reported seeing Kabar, the Great Dane that once belonged to Rudolph Valentino, which died in 1929.

A Poetic Tribute to a Dog Called Boatswain

During the summer months, thousands of visitors flock to Newstead Abbey, the ancestral Nottinghamshire home of Lord Byron, the great poet, philosopher and freedom fighter. My visit was out of season when visitors were outnumbered by peacocks; in fact, as I got out of my car, I was greeted by a peacock's raucous cry that would have set my teeth on edge after dark.

I was in search of the grave of a dog called Boatswain who had belonged to Byron, so I asked directions from a member of staff who pointed me in the right direction. I told him the reason for my visit and asked if he could confirm or deny the stories I had heard about Byron's dog haunting the grounds.

'Oh yes, that's right,' he confirmed. 'Jenny, one of our staff members, was walking through the gardens only a short time ago and sensed a presence behind her. When she felt something brush up against her leg the way dogs do if they pass very close, she felt quite a relief knowing it was only Boatswain.'

I suppose I was expecting to find a tombstone in a distant corner of the park, but no, this is a monument of massive scale standing in majestic isolation in a prime location that can be seen from all areas of the garden. To reach it, I mounted five stone steps and even then it was taller than me, a solid square of stone with a slab of white marble on each side and a hipped roof topped with an urn finial. On two of the marble slabs is this rather rambling verse which, like the monument, is rather pretentious for a dog, but then it was penned by Byron!

A peacock in the grounds of Newstead Abbey.

Boatswain's memorial.

Near this spot are deposited the remains of one who possessed beauty without vanity; strength without insolence, courage without ferocity, and all the virtues of man without his vices. This praise which would be unmeaning flattery if inscribed over human ashes is but a just tribute to the memory of

BOATSWAIN, A DOG

who was born in Newfoundland May 1803
and died at Newstead, November 18th 1808.
When some proud son of man returns to earth
Unknown to Glory but upheld by birth
The sculptor's art exhausts the pomp of woe
And storied urns record who rests below
When all is done upon the Tomb is seen
Not what he was, but what he should have been
But the poor dog, in life the firmest friend
The first to welcome, foremost to defend
Whose honest heart is still his master's own
Who labours, fights, lives, breathes for him alone
Unhonoured falls, unnoticed all his worth
Deny'd in heaven the Soul he had on earth:
While man, vain insect! hopes to be forgiven
And claims himself a sole exclusive heaven
Oh man! Thou feeble tenant of an hour
Debased by slavery, or corrupt by power
Who knows thee well, must quilt thee with disgust

Degraded mass of animated dust
Thy love is lust, thy friendship all a cheat
Thy tongue hypocrisy, thy heart deceit
By nature vile, ennobled but by name
Each kindred brute might bid thee blush with shame
Ye! Who behold perchance this simple urn
Pass on, it honours none you wish to mourn
To mark a friend's remains, these stones arise
I never knew but one — and here he lies

Lord Byron Takes a Ride

A woman was walking through Newstead Abbey Park many years ago. Dusk was turning to darkness and it was raining heavily when she heard the low lament of voices carried on the wind. The sound grew nearer and in the fading light she could see two figures on horseback. One was a man the other a woman but neither appeared to notice her. Their horses' hooves made no sound, and the couple seemed unaffected by the rain as they passed before her and straight through a hedge.

The woman hurried over to the hedge, but on the other side there was no sign of either horses or riders and, even more strange, the hedge was intact and showed no indication of anything or anyone passing through. She examined the ground but all she could see were her own footprints on the muddy path and no evidence of horses' hooves.

Was it her imagination or had the years momentarily slipped away to allow her to see the shade of Lord Byron and his true love, his half-sister Augusta Leigh?

The Working Horse

Around fifty years ago, Edna Thomas was walking along a country path near her home in Shoeburyness, Essex when she sensed the breathing of a horse nearby. It was panting as if pulling a heavy load, and she could hear its hooves on the gravel, but as she looked around she could see nothing. Later she discovered that the area had been a brick field and horses had been used to pull the brick-laden carts along tracks at the exact place she had felt the horse's presence.

Ronald Reagan Rides Again

According to a recent newspaper report, the late President Ronald Reagan has returned to Rancho del Cierlo, his mountain spread near Santa Barbara, California. Visitors to the estate, which is still maintained as he left it, say they have seen a spectral figure in a traditional cowboy outfit riding a horse around the property. It is certainly no-one who works on the 688-acre estate and the description matches that of the ex-president, who in his heyday as a Hollywood actor played many cowboy roles.

The Disappearing Horse

Mabel Hickinson and her friend Frances Smith were walking along the Hathersage to Bamford road. They had reached an area known as Sicklehome Hollow when Frances pointed out a white horse in the field. Mabel looked where Frances was pointing but could see nothing and there were no horses anywhere around. Mabel tried to convince Frances that it was a trick of the light, but she was equally adamant that there was definitely a horse in the field. The argument was settled when they both heard a ghostly neigh and according to Frances the horse simply disappeared.

A spectral horse was seen in this field on the Hathersage to Bamford Road.

The Haunted Intersection

A busy intersection on the edge of the forest preserve of a Chicago suburb is a notorious accident black spot. A rise obscures the driver's view of any individuals attempting to cross the street and quite a number of people have been injured and at least seven have been killed here, including some horses.

There are stables nearby and horse-riding trails cross the dangerous intersection to continue on the other side, although some never make it.

But this is a double accident spot due not only to the actual crossing but because ghostly re-enactments of actual events are claimed to occur here. There have been numerous incidents at night or near dusk of motorists seeing what appears to be a rider in silhouette attempting to cross the road. They are usually seen from afar and described as a smoky grey silhouette with no recognisable features, but as the driver slows down, suddenly there is nothing there.

Even more scarily, in one case a driver reported seeing a rider being thrown from his horse into the middle of the road. On another occasion, a horse was seen being dragged along the road as though a car had impacted with it and dragged or pushed the creature.

The Phantom Horse and Jockey

In 1927, a resident of Newmarket, the East Anglian town famous for its racecourse, declared that she had seen the ghost of the great jockey Fred Archer mounted on his favourite grey horse. The woman was adamant that it was Archer, winner of more than 2,500 races, even though he had been dead for forty years.

According to the woman and her daughter who both saw the apparition, the horse and jockey emerged from a copse, galloped noiselessly towards them, then vanished mysteriously. Other

A phantom horse and jockey were seen at Newmarket.

local people also claim to have seen the phantom horse and jockey in the vicinity of Hamilton Stud Lane and also on the heath. Ten years ago, stable lads at Falmouth stables, where Archer lived for the latter period of his short life, saw his ghost in a room above the stables. This is where Fred, at the age of twenty-nine, shot himself after his wife had died giving birth to their daughter and he was diagnosed with typhoid.

Many people think it is Archer's ghost who is responsible for a number of unexplained mishaps on the Newmarket course where there have been many instances of horses swerving, slowing down or stumbling for no apparent reason. In 1950, jockey Charlie Smirke said he could not explain why his mount, the Aga Khan's horse Kermanshah, fell in a race at a spot where another horse had fallen the previous year. Even more surprising, jockeys and spectators have reported seeing a white formless shape at about the height of a horse's head, hovering in the air at this point.

The Ghost of the Last Bear in England

According to legend, Verdley Woods, just south of Fernhurst near Haslemere, West Sussex was the place where the last bear in England was killed one Christmas day. The bear sought refuge in the Great Hall of Verdley Castle, now a ruin, after being cornered by yokels who discovered the poor beast foraging for food in the snow. Since then, supposedly on Christmas day, the growls of the cornered beast and the shouts of the yokels are still heard there.

This legend obviously appealed to an Australian television crew from Storyteller Media Group who, along with six psychic mediums and two historians, set out in 2005 to search for the legendary ghost of the last bear in England. Whether the spirit creature materialised for the camera is doubtful, because they don't tend to perform to order.

The Ghost of the Daisy Dog

In the sixteenth century intrepid explorers from Portugal and England were discovering new lands and continents, one being the Far East. Trade followed and Queen Elizabeth I was regularly presented with strange and exotic finds from these other worlds. It is therefore not surprising that from this time comes the Cornish legend of the Daisy Dog, reputedly sent as a 'tribute dog' or gift from the Emperor of China.

For over 1,000 years, the orient have produced a number of snub-nosed breeds like the Pekingese and these little dogs were cherished. They were the pets and playthings of nobility, carried in the sleeve of Chinese robes and not seen outside their home lands. It was therefore a very treasured gift to honour our queen with a pair of these little dogs and with them was sent a royal princess.

The voyage was hazardous but the little Pekingese bitch managed to produce a litter en route. The last stage of the journey was even more gruelling and rumours began to circulate amongst the

A pair of little snub-nosed Pekingese dogs were sent as a tribute gift to Queen Elizabeth I.

crew that the princess was a witch intent upon drowning them all. The men mutinied, killed the captain and while several men threw the unfortunate princess overboard, another man took hold of the box containing the dogs, but before he could throw it overboard one of the dogs bit him.

The princess and the box containing the dogs were eventually washed up on a Cornish beach, where a local man found them. The princess was dead, but inside her loose-fitting sleeve something was moving. It was the male Pekingese. The little dog watched as the man opened the box and took out the dead bitch and the puppies. He buried them, planted a cross of daisies on top, then picked up the male dog and placed him gently on top of the grave. The dog licked his hand in gratitude, then lay down and died.

Since then, the ghost of the male Pekingese has been seen wandering aimlessly around the grave. Initially it was rumoured that the ghost of the little dog was guarding buried treasure but as the bitten sailor had died a slow and agonising death, no-one dared to find out. Over the centuries the grave has been left undisturbed as it is believed that if the ghost of the little dog bites you, an excruciating death will follow.

The White Doe

About a mile from West Grinstead there are the remains of Knepp Castle. According to the local legend, in the days of King John, one of the king's retainers was so annoyed when a young girl refused to submit to his advances that he paid a witch to turn her into a white doe. The hunters of Knepp had strict instructions never to kill the little doe, but one day a youth, anxious to display his skills with the crossbow, sent an arrow through its heart, killing it on the spot.

But the ghost of the little doe returned to Knepp Castle and is still seen feeding on the rich grass in summer time, although in winter blood-red marks appear on the frozen snow where the little doe died.

The Ghostly White Hare

At Looe in Cornwall a white hare is said to run down the hill and vanish at the door of an old hostelry named the Jolly Tar Inn. Some tales say the form is that of a witch, others say it is the unhappy spirit of a girl who committed suicide on the premises and now haunts the place. Those who promote the witch story say the mysterious white hare vanishes before she can be caught, but if she is ever caught she will turn back into a witch. What both stories agree on is that the appearance of the ghostly white hare always forecasts impending disaster.

In the Middle Ages when witchcraft was rife the hare, like the cat, was thought to be a favourite shape adopted by witches. Supposedly if a hunter wounded a hare, then later saw a local woman wounded in the same part of the body, this was considered proof that she had changed shape and was therefore a witch. Some tales even tell of hunters killing hares that metamorphosed back into human corpses. This shape-changing or shape-shifting is the stuff of fairytales too. We were weaned on folktales of witches casting spells and turning people into animals. Remember the *Frog Prince*, and the handsome prince transformed into the beast by a wicked witch in *Beauty and the Beast*?

Witches had such power that their influence is even seen in various phrases we still use today. The expression 'having kittens', which tends to apply to women tormented by some irrepressible fear, dates back to the medieval belief that witches could perform a spell on a pregnant woman and turn her baby into kittens. The fear that gripped the mother-to-be would have been unimaginable, but now in our enlightened age we are just left with this strange saying.

In the world of myths, magic and make-believe, things are not always what they seem. The legends of many cultures refer to deities changing into animal form and animals disguising themselves as humans. But changing shape was always a risky business. When the Greek hunter Actaeon watched the goddess Artemis bathing in a lake, she was so furious she changed him into a deer and he was torn to pieces by his own hounds.

According to mythology, the Celtic goddess Epona sometimes appears as a horse, but is more often portrayed riding side-saddle or standing between two foals. The name Epona gives us the word 'pony' and derives from Epos, the Celtic word for horse.

Other creatures are half-human, half-animal, like the god Pan who is depicted as being half-human, half-goat; the half-man, half-horse centaurs and their relatives, the shaggy goat-like satyrs. The list goes on and on, in stories that have been told since ancient times and as we move into the next section, perhaps fuelled by our worst fears.

A young girl who was turned into a white doe now haunts Knepp Castle.

VIII

BLACK DOGS AND GHOSTLY HOUNDS

Black dogs are the most frequently sighted ghostly animals. Also referred to as demon dogs, they are usually ominous and go out of their way to convey to anyone meeting them that they are monsters from beyond the grave.

There are so many accounts of these dogs that they are treated as something of a phenomena in their own right. Stretching the length and breadth of Britain it is virtually impossible to even start to comprehend the widespread nature of the subject, but all have one thing in common; they are believed to be omens of bad luck and said to presage death. This idea may be linked to the black dog's connection with the devil, who purportedly assumed the shape of a large black dog at witches' orgiastic gatherings or sabbats.

Stanton Moor in Derbyshire is an area rich in stone circles, burial mounds and other remnants of our ancient past. It is also at the junction of many ley lines, and is reputed to be haunted by a spectral black dog with flaming eyes, huge teeth and a foaming mouth. Some people believe that these spectral dogs only run on ley lines.

According to the *Daily Express* dated October 1925, Edale, a few miles north of Stanton Moor, was terrorised by a creature of enormous size, black in colour and possessing a howl like a foghorn. One eyewitness is reported as saying, 'It sat on its haunches and it was bigger than me'.

In Budleigh Hill in Somerset, a black dog with fiery eyes as big as saucers has been seen. A similar description is given of Barguest, the black dog of Trollers Gill in Yorkshire. The black dog of Lancashire is called Trash and in the north of England the black dog is known as the Padfoot. It reputedly has huge saucer eyes and backward-pointing feet. In Burnley there is Shriker or Tach, a large shaggy animal with broad feet that make a splashing sound as it walks.

A black, shaggy animal about the size of a pony with red or green glowing eyes is the description given of Old Shock, the Suffolk name for the black dog. Shock and Shuck come from the Anglo-Saxon word *scucca*, meaning demon, and Black Shuck is a Norfolk black dog with just a single eye that burns like a lantern. Shuck is also the ancient name used around Coventry. Here, place names like Hounds Hill, Dog Land, Upper Shuckmoor and Lower Shuckmoor go back to the fourteenth century and relate to the stamping ground of the beast.

In Herefordshire there is a Shucknall; at Crich near Matlock there is a Shuckwood, Shuckstone Lane and Shuckstone field. Only the base of Shuckstone Cross remains on the hilltop above Lea but the strange symbols carved round the top, although indecipherable, make it rather unusual. At Mercaston near Brailsford in south Derbyshire there is a Shuckton Manor, a Grade-II Listed property built in 1729 on the site of an older building. The house stands on an elevated site in

A ghostly black dog?

an area of outstanding natural beauty surrounded by rolling countryside, yet the name would imply that it is, or has been, the province of a shuck.

A farmhand was leading two carthorses along a country lane in Coventry early one morning when a large shaggy black dog came padding down the lane towards them. The boy and horses froze in their tracks as the creature passed through a hedge and disappeared in a flash of white light.

A lorry driver and his mate were driving along a rural road when out of the bushes came a black dog. It seemed oblivious to the lorry and strolled across the road, causing the driver to brake suddenly. Then it turned its head towards the lorry and both men stared in disbelief. The dog was like a silhouette with no features – no nose, mouth or eyes – then suddenly it just disappeared.

A farmer in Dorset heard an animal behind him and turned to see a large black dog with a stream of sulphurous vapour pouring from its throat. In Somerset a black dog haunts the road from St Audies to Perry Farm, and in Buckinghamshire a farmer struck out in the dark at the glowing eyes of a black dog which instantly disappeared. A Devon farmer chased a black dog that exploded in a blinding flash, so is it surprising that where the dog has roamed there is supposedly a smell of brimstone and burning?

If you should meet one, don't strike it, because like a ball of energy, it will ignite. In Essex, the driver of a wagon struck out at a large black dog that exploded, setting him and his wagon on fire. In Coventry, a horseman was returning home from an inn in Keresley when a snarling black dog confronted him. No doubt shocked by its sudden appearance, he is said to have struck it with his riding crop, at which point it exploded in a flash, blowing the rider off his horse and the clothes off his back. The traumatised horse was eventually found two days later.

A Tale of the Norfolk Shuck

This is a tale told by a Yarmouth sailor around 1933 and relates to his great- grandfather who came from Potter Higham and used to drive a pony round the countryside selling fish. He always travelled in daylight as the deep water either side of some of the roads made them treacherous after dark when there was always the likelihood of meeting a phantom coach or worst of all, the Shuck.

One night he was late returning home. It was early winter and the moon was up. The old pony, a Norfolk trotter, was making a good pace for home when something black jumped out of the hedge and into the back of the cart.

The Shuck terrorises country districts.

The dog whip at Baslow church.

The pony took fright and ran, and the man took one look and yelled because sitting behind him amongst the fish and breathing in his ears was the Black Shuck. He was described as being as big as a calf or donkey and his eyes lit up like lamps.

They took the road like a streak of lightning but when they had to turn a corner, the whole cart turned over and the man was pitched out on his head. As soon as it was light, his two sons went out to search for him and found the cart in bits. The pony had limped home and from that day onward, neither of them ever did another day's work.

Sometimes these dog-like creatures that terrorise travellers on lonely lanes are referred to as boggarts. The name is related to 'barghast', from the German 'geist' or ghost and has come to imply a troublesome ghost or spirit.

Daniel Cohen's *Encyclopaedia of Ghosts* tells of the black dog that haunted the Vaughan family. When one of the children contracted smallpox, his mother rushed downstairs to instruct her husband to drive away the large black dog that was lying on the child's bed. She was not aware of the legend of the black dog, but her husband was, and fearing the worse, he ran upstairs. The child was already dead.

There are numerous reports of a phantom black dog at Peel Castle on the Isle of Man where a black dog supposedly haunts the underground passageway near the guardrooms. Although they normally gave it a wide berth, one day a guardsman entered the guardroom alone and was so traumatised by what he saw that he could only gasp as he fell into unconsciousness. Naturally this further fuelled the belief that the dog was a harbinger of death.

Sax Rohmer, creator of the fictional detective Fu Manchu, spent a night in Peel Castle to investigate the phenomena. He reported hearing dog-like howls coming from inside the blocked-up passageway where a guardroom had once been and believed that the dog dated from the time of early pagan rituals. A dog was incorporated into the walls of early buildings in the belief that it would protect the place from evil.

There have been reports of a headless black dog that haunts the humpback bridge at Ivelet in Swaledale. The bridge lies on the Corpse Way, the path used for bringing the dead down to the church. The dog apparently glides onto the bridge and disappears over the edge.

What most of these dogs have in common is their ability to disappear instantly, but there is always an exception, like this incident in Manchester. A man called Drabble encountered a headless black dog outside an old church. The dog leapt up, putting his paws on the terrified man's shoulders, but as he turned and ran the dog gave chase.

The market weathervane in Bungay, Suffolk denotes a demonic black dog, wide-eyed and slavering, and relates to an incident that happened on Sunday 4 August 1577. When most of the townsfolk were at prayer in the twelfth-century church of St Mary, a huge black dog entered the church and ran down the central aisle killing two people and injuring a third. According to

The snarling black dog was something to be reckoned with.

legend, its claws burnt into the wood of the church door and tore at the stonework, marks that are still visible today.

Coincidentally, a similar story is attached to the nearby church at Blythburgh, where three people were killed. In fact the practice must have been quite universal because many churches up and down the country employed dog-whippers to keep stray animals out of church.

For several hundred years, the church warders' account at Youlgreave in Derbyshire included the salary of the dog-whipper. It states – *for whipping ye dogges forthe of ye churche in tyme of divyne service.* For performing this duty in 1609, Herbert Walton received sixteen pence.

It is perhaps not surprising that all the whips have disappeared from our churches, yet at Baslow church in Derbyshire a dog whip is still preserved in a glass-fronted wooden case that hangs just inside the door. It would appear that this church is still having problems with wildlife slipping inside as a notice on the door states - *Please come in. Help keep the birds and bats out. Do close the door. Thank you.*

If a dog was heard howling, it supposedly forecast death, but in our enlightened age an alternative theory is that the dog had rabies, also known as canine madness, which rejects the supernatural assumption entirely.

When a dog suffers from this disease, it howls and whines and makes strange noises that people can't fail to notice. If a rabid dog bit its owner, who then died, stories would circulate that the owner met with death not long after the dog was heard making unusual noises. In an era before the transmission of infection was understood, it is possible to see how the dog's cries could be interpreted as a forewarning of human death. Dogs suffering from rabies were hanged or struck on the head, and rabies was eradicated from Britain in 1903.

And just to show that there is always an exception to every rule, in Norfolk and Suffolk, the Shuck is just as likely to be white. For this reason, in days gone by, they drowned all white dogs because they believed they brought bad luck and flooding. In the 1950s it was believed that prior to the bad floods that caused such devastation along that coastline, a pack of white dogs had been seen running along the harbour at Harwich.

Cerberus
Perhaps these tales of hellhounds all originate from the Greek and Roman myths in which a fierce three-headed dog called Cerberus guarded the entrance to Hades, the Greek underworld, otherwise known as Hell. This three-headed dog had the tail of a dragon, a thick mane of hissing, writhing snakes and its fangs dripped poison.

Its counterpart in Egypt was Anubis, the dog who guarded the tombs, and Garm, a similar dog that guarded the house of death in Norse mythology. Cerberus was the offspring of Echidna, a half-woman/half-serpent, (which would account for its mane) and the dragon Typhon (which would account for its tail) and had a brother named Orthrus or Orphus which was also a monstrous dog with two heads.

Ancient Greek and Romans placed a coin and a small cake in the hands of their deceased; the coin was meant as payment for Charon, who ferried the souls across the river Styx, and the cake was to pacify Cerberus.

Cerberus was overcome several times, leaving Hell's gates unguarded and the final labour of Heracles was to capture Cerberus and bring it from the underworld. He did this by treating it with the first kindness it had ever received, a monster story with a moral message.

In *Harry Potter and the Philosopher's Stone*, there is a giant three-headed dog named Fluffy that guards the Philosopher's Stone. It could be lulled to sleep by playing it music, as Orpheus lulled Cerberus to sleep with his musical skills when he made the journey to the underworld to bring back his lover, Eurydice.

The Big Cats
Menacing black dogs have been reported for centuries, yet since a puma was sighted forty years ago in Surrey, there have been reports that hundreds of menacing big cats are also on the prowl in the UK. The British Big Cat Society have on record 2,123 sightings of pumas, panthers, lynxes and other big cats, sighted in a fifteen-month period between April 2004 and July 2005.

Devon had the most sightings with 132, Yorkshire 127, Scotland 125 and Wales with 123, Gloucester and Sussex had 104 each, while Kent, Cornwall, Somerset and Leicester all had over 90. Danny Bamping, who founded the society, believes many of these big cats were once exotic pets released when their owners lost interest, others may have escaped from zoos or may be members of cat families assumed to be extinct in Britain. So far there have been no reports of a paranormal nature.

The Hellhound of Beccles
On the lonely lane leading to her home on the outskirts of Beccles, Suffolk, sixteen-year-old Amy Castile heard a soft growl and slowly an enormous, semi-transparent hound emerged from the hedge. For a moment they stared at each other then the hound trotted quickly away. This was the third time Amy had seen it but no-one believed her story until one day she and her mother were returning from shopping in the nearby town of Bungay.

It was getting dark as they entered the lane and Amy became agitated as she heard the distinct growl that she knew forecast the hound's appearance. She was not wrong. A minute later, the massive black hound appeared, yet still Mrs Castile could see nothing.

'It's there by the holly hedge,' screamed Amy, grabbing her mother's hand, and almost immediately Mrs Castile saw the looming shape of the animal. She stared in disbelief at the almost transparent dog, but as Amy removed her hand, the hound vanished from her sight completely.

After this, Morley Adams, a psychic investigator, was called in. He managed to persuade Amy to spend half an hour at dusk with him at the place she had seen the hound emerge from the hedge, and although on the first occasion nothing happened, on the second evening, Morley felt Amy stiffen in terror.

Although he could neither hear nor see anything, for reassurance he placed his hand firmly on Amy's and immediately he too saw the massive black hound, which stared at them with bared fangs. He pulled his hand away and instantly the image and sound disappeared, yet as soon as he touched Amy's hand again the dog reappeared to him. It advanced a few paces towards them before turning and trotting away.

Next day Morley obtained permission to dig in the field behind the hedge and by mid-afternoon he had unearthed the remains of a hessian sack containing the bones of a huge dog. Later Morley discovered that a six-year-old girl who had lived at the Castile cottage thirty years previously had been mauled by a huge dog. She had died of her injuries and her distraught father had taken his own revenge by killing the dog and burying it.

Amy's psychic power was able to bring the hound from its grave and her clairvoyant ability was so strong that by touching her, even people without her power were able to see the hound too.

The Superstitious Miner and the Black Dog

Derbyshire lead miners had many superstitions, and seeing a black dog prowling round old mine workings and soughs was considered a very bad omen. A story from Bradwell near Castleton tells how a miner and his mate were returning home one moonlit evening when the miner was terrified by the sudden appearance of a large black dog. The strange thing was, only he could see the dog, even as it approached and passed under their feet. He was so convinced that the dog was an omen of bad luck that he refused to go down the mine the following day. His disbelieving colleague did and was killed when the roof fell on him.

The Black Dogs at the Graves

In December 1745 Prince Charles Edward Stewart, better known as Bonnie Prince Charlie, and his Jacobite soldiers reached Derby, the furthest point south on their unsuccessful attempt to re-establish the Stuart succession. After heated discussions, the decision was made to withdraw.

All the men were recalled and began their long trek back to Scotland, but many never left the area. The dispirited army was an easy target for ambush and death. Many Jacobite soldiers were slain and buried where they fell and around the Leek/Ashbourne area there have been reports of a phantom black dog guarding their wayside graves.

The Sight and Sound of Ghostly Hounds

When the Vikings invaded England, they brought with them many Norse myths that quickly spread around the north of England. One such legend told of the Hounds of Odin, believed to take the form of terrifying spirits who served Odin as war-dogs. These were also known as Hounds of the Underworld or Otherworld, the regions below the earth's surface regarded as the abode of the dead, and some believe that the lead dog is the devil himself.

Hounds baying at the moon.

The origin of the folklore of these hunting hounds could also stem from ancient Greece when the goddess Diana was associated with spectral hounds hunting for lost souls. Diana was believed to ride on the back of a hound as she rode across the moonlit sky. Mythology tells of the 'wild hunt', a pack of spectral hounds who glide through the air on stormy nights led by a figure on a white horse. Often this phantom aerial hunt was heard and not seen.

Some people believe that these ghostly hunting hounds are only seen at key times of the year. Dando and his dogs were believed to roam Cornwall and appear only on Sundays. Dando was a priest who was fond of the excesses of life including alcohol and hunting. It is said that he was out on a hunt when he needed a drink to satisfy his binge, so he shouted, 'I'd go to hell for a draft'. Suddenly a figure, thought to be the devil, appeared and offered him a drink, but as he accepted it, Dando was said to have burst into flames and disappeared.

The Rach hounds, also known as Gabriel's hounds, in North Derbyshire, are heard but never seen. The howling of these animals is said to presage death or disaster.

A phantom huntsman and hounds has been seen at Bretton Clough, a secluded wooded valley that divides the two heather-covered uplands of Eyam Moor and Offerton Moor in Derbyshire. A lady and her companion who had no knowledge of this phantom hunt heard a hunting horn here during the 1930s.

Cwn Annwn is a hunt believed to be an omen of death or great disaster according to ancient Welsh tradition. The howling of the hounds was said to decrease as the hunt approached and ultimately the sound was no more than a single dog panting as it settled near a place or person. Once the hound had signalled the death of someone, it would swiftly move away and, as it did so, the sound would begin to increase until the horrific howls were terrifying.

According to legend the ghost of Sir Frances Drake (1545-96) has been seen on Dartmoor riding with a pack of spectral hounds whose cries are so terrible that any dog hearing them is frightened to death. It is also said that Drake's ghost sets off for Plymouth from Tavistock in a black coach or hearse, drawn by four headless horses.

At Haltwhistle, Northumberland near the remains of the old Roman wall, a phantom hunt has been seen galloping past. The neighbourhood's terrified dogs and cats supposedly run for miles to get away from these spectral hounds.

Windsor Great Park has long been reputed to be haunted by the ghost of Herne the Hunter whose great shaggy form is usually glimpsed at night-time amongst ancient trees. The apparition wears horns and is mounted on a fast horse followed by spectral hounds. The whole ghostly band is seemingly engaged on a phantom hunting expedition.

The original Herne was a forest keeper in Great Windsor Forest, probably in the reign of Richard II. Falling from grace, he hung himself from an oak tree. The ghost of Herne and his phantom hounds have been reported from various parts of Windsor Great Park, the sound is heard suddenly, then gradually fades away. One resident heard the baying of hounds coming from the direction of Smith's Lawn. It appeared to increase in volume then die away in the area around Windsor Castle.

Herne's Horn

This is a very old folk tale that has been brought up to date with present-day characters, two boys from Windsor and a visiting vandal, intent upon causing destruction in Windsor Great Park. They were breaking down young trees when the visitor found a horn hidden in the undergrowth.

'Look what I've found,' he called waving the horn. 'I'd say someone's been filming Robin Hood round here.'

The two Windsor boys looked visibly shaken. 'Put it back,' said one.

'Don't touch it,' shouted the other and started to run away. The other boy followed but the visitor had to try out the horn and took a good blow. It gave a groan then a blast and suddenly there was a terrible yell amongst the trees and the sound of great hounds baying.

The lad dropped the horn and ran, but he was way behind the Windsor lads who were making for the church. Run as he might, he kept stumbling.

The Windsor lads, safe in the church, saw him run and stagger and they heard the dogs baying. He was nearly at the door when they heard the twang of an arrow and the boy screamed, threw up his arms, and fell flat on his face, quite dead, yet there was no arrow, no hunter and no hounds.

The Hound of the Baskervilles

The most famous story of a ghostly hound must be Sir Arthur Conan Doyle's *Hound of the Baskervilles*. It is said that this story was influenced by tales of the headless 'Yell Hound' that only appears during twilight hours to hunt either a person or a spirit.

Set on Dartmoor in Devon in 1889, the Baskerville family was cursed by a legend that went back to 1650 and Sir Hugo Baskerville who made a pact to 'sell his soul to the devil for a wench'. Shortly afterwards, his body was found torn to shreds, purportedly by a huge, supernatural hound. Every heir since had met a similar, sudden, mysterious and violent death. This destructive curse was finally foiled thanks to the deductive skills of Sherlock Holmes who found that a neighbour called Jack Stapleton had reinvented the legend of the hound to get rid of the Baskervilles. Once they were eliminated, as a distant relative, Jack Stapleton intended to claim inheritance of Baskerville Hall and its lands, and no doubt squash the legend that had helped him attain them.

IX

SPECTRAL HORSES

In pre-mechanical days, the horse was extremely valuable to its owner, both as a form of transport and as a draught animal, so the horse was seen as a prime target for any evil witch wanting to bring harm or disruption. Many farmers believed that witches could stop a working team of horses and keep them in a suspended state until they decided to let them start up again. Witches were also thought capable of casting spells to make a horse go lame, become ill or even die and because of this, horse-owners safeguarded their animals by surrounding them with things that were traditionally thought to ward off evil. This was the origin of horse brasses, now seen as adornment in many country pubs. By hanging brass bells or shiny horse brasses on working horses, it was believed that this would keep at bay any witches or familiars who would be dazzled by the brightness of the objects.

For protection the rider, or the driver of a team of horses, would carry a whip made with a branch from a favourite anti-witch tree, the rowan or mountain ash. They would hang a horseshoe or a piece of rowan on the stable door, and round the horse's neck would be hung a stone with a hole in it, known as a hagstone, or witch-stone.

From an era when horses and horse power were the only means of transport comes a selection of stories of people being carried around on ghostly horses. People have witnessed highwaymen and soldiers astride their fast horses, and visitors staying at old coaching inns have been woken in the night by the sound of ghostly mail coaches rumbling into the courtyard. There are many accounts of the sound of spectral hooves, the shouts of riders and the baying of the hounds that often accompany the horses, and just in case you should come across one, beware of those ghostly death coaches pulled by headless horses that scoop up the unsuspecting observer.

Haunted Crossroads

It is often noted that horses react very strangely when approaching crossroads because, unknown to many riders, the horse is probably sensing spirits. The ancient Greeks and Romans left offerings of food at crossroads to make sure the hell-hounds did not attack dead souls. The favourite offering was a dead dog.

Crossroads have always been believed to be a favourite haunt of ghosts, one theory being that witches held orgies and practised the black arts there and, in doing so, conjured up strange apparitions. Suspect witches, murderers and suicides were buried at crossroads, not only to accentuate their marginal status in society, but in the Christian belief that the cross would offer a form of protection for the living against the demons, vampires and supernatural night creatures

A rare photograph of a ghost horse?

The sound of trotting horses has been heard coming up the south drive at Bolsover Castle.

that would manifest round these unfortunates. Then, just to be on the safe side, many were buried with a stake thrust through their bodies in the belief that this would keep their spirits from wandering.

One such incident happened in 1810, when a young man named Geoffrey Wood took his own life. As was the custom of the time, his body was transported on a horse-drawn cart and buried without ceremony at a rural road junction just outside Coventry, but since then many people have reported seeing the ghostly reconstruction of this event. A man is seen to lead a horse and cart towards the crossroads, yet the horse walks without making any sound, there is no rumble from the cart and as they reach the crossroad they simply melt into the ground.

Bolsover's Ghostly Horses

Sir William Cavendish had a pre-occupation with all things equestrian and belonged to an elite group of horsemen skilled in ceremonial tournaments. He built the riding house at Bolsover Castle to enable him to show off his skills and his ghost may still be there doing just that. In the riding house, the sound of horses has been heard by security guards; strange lights move around as if someone is carrying a candle and the electrical equipment, recordings and lights switch themselves off and on.

Walking around the castle, many visitors hear the sound of marching feet and trotting horses coming up the south drive.

This could be blamed on the strange acoustic properties of the area but people who have heard them believe them to be the ghosts of Sir William's Whitecoats returning from their Civil War defeat at Marston Moor.

The Sound of a Ghostly Cavalry

On 4 December 1745, Prince Charles Edward Stuart, better known as Bonnie Prince Charlie, accompanied by a bodyguard of Scottish lords, the music of bagpipes and an army of 7,000, reached Derby. He was leading the Jacobite Rebellion on their march to London in an attempt to re-establish the Stuart succession.

While most of the army were billeted around Derby, a group of seventy Scottish soldiers were sent on to Swarkstone, seven miles south, to secure Swarkstone Bridge, the only way of crossing the River Trent. Meanwhile heated discussion took place at Exeter House in Derby. Charles wanted to continue the march south but his officers wanted to retreat and eventually, in desperation, Charles had to accept defeat as the decision was made to abandon their attempt to re-establish the Stuart succession and Charles's dream of taking the English crown from George II.

On 6 December all the soldiers were recalled and began their long march back to Scotland. But have they left a lasting legacy? Around Swarkstone Bridge, many people report hearing the sound of horses' hooves and the accompanying clatter of armour and swords, although the ghostly cavalry never materialise.

According to one report, 'I could hear the galloping hooves of horses growing louder and louder behind me, but whenever I turned to look, all I could see was empty air. The sound grew so loud as if it was coming right at me, passed through me, then carried on, growing more distant and loosing volume as it went further away. The whole experience lasted only about three minutes from the time I first heard the distant hoof beats to the time when they had passed through me and faded away again. It was not an echo and there could be no other natural explanation.'

The Headless Peddler

A phantom white horse with a headless rider is said to gallop through the Manifold Valley on moonlit nights. It is alleged to be the ghost of a peddler, murdered by two men who cut off his head and set his headless body back on his horse and drove it across the moors. An awful gory sight it must be, but at least this is one incident when we can account for why the rider is headless.

The Phantom Horse of Beeley Moors

It is said that on the first night of the full moon in March, the ghost of a rider on a black horse can be seen and heard galloping over the Derbyshire moors.

Four hundred years ago, despite a desperate search by distraught husband and father Henry Columbell, a woman and her children froze to death in a blizzard on the bleak Beeley Moors of Derbyshire. Apparently poor Henry still continues his fruitless search galloping round the area calling his wife's name.

The concept of ghost horses has always been strong, and around forty years ago a popular song reflected the idea of ghost riders in the sky. The words, although aimed at the lone cowboy, have a message for everyone.

> An old cowpoke went riding out one dark and windy day
> Upon a ridge he rested as he went along his way
> When all at once a mighty herd of red-eyed cows he saw
> A'plowin' through the ragged skies and up a cloudy draw
> Their brands were still on fire and their hooves were made of steel
> Their horns wuz black and shiny and their hot breaths he could feel
> A bolt of fear went through him as they thundered through the sky
> For he saw the riders comin' hard and he heard their mournful cry
> Their faces gaunt, their eyes were blurred and shirts all soaked with sweat
> They're riding hard to catch that herd but they ain't caught them yet
> They've got to ride forever in that range up in the sky
> On horses snorting fire, as they ride on hear their cry
> As the riders loped on by him, he heard one call his name
> 'If you want to save your soul from hell a' ridin' on our range
> Then cowboy change your ways today or with us you will ride
> A-tryin' to catch the devil's herd across these endless skies
> Yi-pi-yi-ay, yi-pi-yi-o
> Ghost riders in the sky

Highwayman's Haunts

The most frequently reported ghostly individual seen on horseback is the highwayman. The archetypal highwayman was born in the aftermath of the Civil War when many Royalist officers were left without any means of support. Although terrorising to travellers, the highwayman was portrayed as a romantic figure astride his powerful horse, an aristocrat amongst thieves, who just happened to be down on his luck. With a reputation greatly enhanced by his gallantry to ladies, his illicit affairs and his numerous narrow escapes, the highwayman soon became a popular folk hero.

The Mysterious Highwayman

Three people were in a car driving just south of Denton, Lincolnshire. It was late and dark, and as the car rounded a bend the driver suddenly saw a dark figure on horseback about to cross his path. He jammed on his brakes to avoid a collision, but as he did so, the figure disappeared. The other surprised occupants of the car had seen nothing, but the driver described a stereo type highwayman dressed in a tricorn hat and cloak.

Night Riding

Friars at Winchelsea, Sussex, the picturesque ruins of an old Franciscan monastery, was once the home of two brothers, George and Joseph Weston. They lived there under assumed names as these country gentlemen were actually highwaymen who plied their nefarious trade throughout the surrounding countryside. Apprehended in London after robbing the Bristol Mail Coach, they were executed at Tyburn in 1782, but their ghosts are still seen careering around the countryside at dead of night astride their fast horses.

Dick Turpin Rides Again

By far the most famous highwayman was Dick Turpin and the whole country seems to be steeped in Turpin folklore. He travelled on such a regular basis that inns were an integral part of his life on the road, and as countless old coaching inns still exist, it is not surprising that many, rather posthumously, claim to have enjoyed his custom, and now his ghost.

Dick Turpin was hung at York on 7 April 1739, but the ghost of the intrepid Dick has purportedly been seen many times making his escape astride his faithful horse Black Bess.

Woodcock Lane, Aspley Guise, Bedfordshire is said to be haunted by the sound of galloping hooves and a phantom on horseback, believed to be the notorious Dick on Black Bess. According to the legend, the daughter of the house had a lover and when they were caught by her father, he imprisoned them in the pantry were he allowed them to slowly starve to death. Many years later, Dick Turpin broke into Woodfield and accidentally discovered the bodies, giving him a perfect excuse for blackmail. From then on, he was allowed to use the house on a regular basis.

People still report hearing the sound of galloping hooves in the vicinity of Woodcock Lane, and there are many reports of a ghostly man on horseback. He apparently dismounts and hurriedly enters the grounds, seemingly through a thick hedge which many years ago, investigation has found, was an entrance to the property.

The Old Cart Tracks

When Derek Acora, the television psychic, walked round an old manor house in Cheshire, he was amazed to see, clairvoyantly, horse-drawn wagons parading backwards and forwards through the living quarters of the old house. Even more bizarre was the fact that he could only see the horses from the belly upwards. Their legs and the lower half of the wagon's wheels were invisible. When he reported his findings to the historian present, he was able to say that the house had been radically altered and extended. What Derek was viewing was the route that the carters used that ran under the foundations of the present building, hence only the upper portion of the horses and carts were visible.

The Phantom Wagon

During the latter part of the 1920s Charles Rackham and a friend were cycling along the Epping Road, near Epping Forest, when they heard the click-clack sound of horses' hooves

Phantom wagons are still seen on our roads and even driving through buildings.

and the creak of a waggon coming up behind them. They pulled over to the side to allow the horse-drawn vehicle to pass and the noise intensified as it carried on past them, but nothing was there.

Mail Coaches

The mail coach era began when post boys on horses were replaced by coaches in 1784. In 1796, sixteen mail coaches came and left London every day, while fifteen more served cross-country routes. By 1811, 220 mail coaches covered over 11,000 miles a day, travelling at a speed of eight miles per hour.

Mail coaches also delivered parcels and passengers. They carried four people inside on two facing seats and three passengers rode on the outside beside and behind the coachman.

The mail coach era thrived until 1836 when the Post Office began to utilise the railways and eventually, for all remote travel, trains replaced horses.

However, there are many phantom coaches dating back to the old coaching days that still haunt their old routes. Many old inns that were on the coaching routes report hearing the mysterious sounds of horses and heavy wheels in cobbled courtyards.

Phantom Death Coaches

The majority of stories of phantom coaches are referred to as death coaches because they are considered to be omens of death. These phantom coaches are customarily black, pulled by headless horses driven at a furious pace by a driver with skeletal or grotesque features. Some people believed they are seen prior to a death in the family, but as their key purpose is to find victims to take to the other side, beware! If anyone gets in the way of a phantom coach they will be carried away to their own doom!

If you happen to be travelling through the Manifold Valley, watch out for the phantom Cromwell Coach. In the daytime, only the sound of its wheels can be heard, but at night its flickering coach-lamps are seen.

The road which runs between Youlgreave and Middleton has a phantom coach and horses lit by eerie lamps and accompanied by ghostly dogs. One witness is said to have felt the wind as it passed.

The Devil's Phantom Coach

A Norfolk legend avows that at midnight on 31 May, a phantom coach races from the hall at Potter Heigham to its destruction on the three-arched bridge in the village. The story dates back to 31 May 1742, when Lady Evelyn Carew married Sir Godfrey Haslitt in Norwich Cathedral, but this union was only made possible because Lady Evelyn made a pact with the devil. She stated that she would be his if only she could be the bride of Sir Godfrey.

Obviously, everything went to plan and the wedding took place, but on the stroke of midnight, the devil claimed his due. The bride was abducted and carried away in a waiting coach occupied by four skeletons and pulled by four black horses. It raced down the drive and headed towards Potter Heigham with its terrified occupant screaming for help. As it reached the narrow bridge in the village, it swung across the road, smashed into the parapet, broke into pieces and fell, horses and all, into the river below. Now, this nightmare apparition it would seem, is re-enacted annually on each anniversary.

Anne's Ghostly Journey

Blickling Hall in Norfolk, the childhood home of Anne Boleyn, has a double haunting that stems from her execution in 1536.

Anne and her brother Lord George Rochfort were beheaded on Tower Green on 19 May and when news of the atrocity reached Blicking Hall, there was seen the grisly apparition of four headless horses racing across the countryside dragging behind them a headless man.

On every anniversary since, a phantom coach drawn by headless horses and driven by a headless coachman reportedly drives to the hall where it vanishes into thin air. Alarming though that is, the coach is reputedly not empty. Inside sits the ghost of Anne Boleyn carrying her head on her knees.

ANNE BOLEYN

Anne Boleyn, the second wife of Henry VIII, was probably born at Blickling. A life-size wooden figure is on the half-landing to the right.

Curious Facts...

Anne Boleyn had an extra finger on one of her hands.

And . . . on the anniversary of her death, she is said to haunt Blickling. A coach drives up to the house, driven by headless horses and a headless coachman, with Anne Boleyn inside, holding her head in her lap!

A part page from the Blickling Hall guidebook.

Mail coaches served the country until 1836.

Bridal Carriage

According to a Derbyshire legend a horse and carriage carrying a bride to her wedding in Ashbourne turned over on Spend Lane. The bride was killed and since then the lane has become an accident black spot where for no apparent reason cars have filled with smoke, horses have panicked and cars have crashed.

Lady Howard's Silent Lament

There is a legend that on certain nights, on the stroke of midnight, the ghost of Lady Howard sets off in her magnificent black coach drawn by four jet-black horses driven by her liveried coachman and accompanied by a large black dog. They drive through the gates of the ruined Fitzford Mansion just outside Tavistock, and take the road to Oakhampton. Motorists have reported seeing the coach rolling silently along the road, and some spectators claim to hear the muffled sound of the horses' hooves and the barely audible noise of the wheels.

The coach is said to stop outside Oakhampton church where the accompanying large black dog plucks a single blade of grass from the churchyard and returns to the coach. Lady Howard takes the grass from the dog's mouth and presses it sadly to her bosom, then the coach turns and heads back to Fitzford Mansion as silently as it came.

The Silent Coach

The old turnpike road from Coventry to Tamworth is haunted by a phantom coach resplendent in all its livery, yet as it sweeps along, there is no sound of horses' hooves or rattle of wheels. People who have seen it say the four horses that pull it are all blinkered and black, apart from one that has a white blaze on its forehead.

The Disappearing Horse and Cart

A Rotherham motorcyclist was riding his motorbike on the road between Bamford and Glossop late one night, when ahead of him in the beam of his headlight he spotted what appeared to be a horse and cart. The cart was an unusual design with high sides and back and as he pulled into the middle of the road to prepare to overtake, he saw the driver walking alongside leading the horse and holding a long whip.

Suddenly, an approaching vehicle with undimmed headlights temporarily blinded the motorcyclist and, when he recovered, he realised that the road ahead of him was deserted.

The road between Bamford and Glossop where a phantom coach has been seen.

Thinking that the horse might have taken fright and plunged off the road down the steep embankment, he got off his bike to search, but there was no sign of the mystery horse and cart.

The Mystery of the Disappearing Lights

Jack Smith was driving home late one evening through the flat, Lincolnshire fen country. The road was so straight, it was possible to see for miles and Jack was just thinking how lonely and desolate the area was when he saw the dim lights of an oncoming vehicle approaching. It was impossible to judge the distance accurately, but the two lights, although dim, were definitely twinkling towards him along the road, so he dipped his headlights courteously. Almost instantaneously the lights vanished, so assuming the vehicle had turned off down a side road, he turned his headlights onto full beam again.

It was only as he drove further that he realised there were no other roads, lanes or cart-tracks turning off the road, and it was then that he began to panic. Had the approaching vehicle accidentally driven off the road? The thought gave him goosebumps and he slowed down so that he could scan the verges either side of the road. When he found nothing, he turned his car round and drove slowly back again. Still he found nothing and decided to report what he was sure was a fatal accident to the local police.

Much to his surprise, they listened patiently, then laughed as they told him he had witnessed the lights of a phantom coach. In the eighteenth century, this coach had apparently got lost in the fog, left the highway and been sucked into a bog. It was not until many years later that the coach, horses and passengers were found, and since then, they have haunted that stretch of road, re-enacting their last, fatal journey.

Phantom coach and horses, similar to the one in this photograph taken in August 1914, regularly appear on some roads.

The Phantom Coach at Cranley

Two hundred years ago, a stagecoach was dashing along Cranley Road, west of Coventry, when it plunged off the road and into a swamp, drowning all its passengers. At a time that was rife with superstition and folklore it was believed that a gigantic, man-eating swamp-beast called Grendel emerged from his bleak watery lair to snatch human and animal victims and drag them down to his cave at the bottom of the lake. Frightening though that might sound, that fatal journey didn't happen just once, it has been re-enacted regularly since.

The galloping hooves of spectral horses have been heard by residents of Cranley Road, and the coach, pulled by four black horses, has been seen on many occasions. In fact sightings have been so numerous that in the 1930s, when a public house was built on the site of the swamp, it was given the name The Phantom Coach.

And so, if you will excuse this deliberately ambiguous statement, this is probably a good place to stop and ponder.

As in all aspects of the paranormal, never before have animal lovers been so keen to penetrate the barriers that separate the world of reality from the mysterious realms of the supernatural. We have looked at animal ghosts in folklore and in our homes, and for the first time in one book have been able to bring together the most sensitive and interesting experiences of a range of pet owners who have so generously shared their secrets and experiences with us.